TRACKSIDE *around* CLEVELAND 1965-1979 *with* Dave McKay

by **Dave McKay**

Library of Congress
Catalog Card No. 2004113803

First Printing
ISBN 1-58248-151-2

Published by
Morning Sun Books, Inc.
9 Pheasant Lane
Scotch Plains, NJ 07076
Printed in Korea

Robert J. Yanosey, President
To access our full library *In Color* visit us at
www.morningsunbooks.com

DEDICATION

In the days before scanners and rail press newsmagazines, it was the tower operators who welcomed the railfan into their work environment and provided the vital information to help him get his photos. I thank so many for their gracious hospitality over the years, in particular Joe and Milt at BE; "Brownie" and Tom R. at QD; Jim Rowe at PE; and Charlie Laird at Sterling.

ACKNOWLEDGEMENTS

Any book project requires input from good friends. First, thanks to Bob Yanosey of Morning Sun Books. It was a phone call from Bob, looking for slides for an unrelated project that initiated this book on the railroads of Cleveland. His continued encouragement and advice on the book has been invaluable. Jeremy Plant read the entire manuscript and provided editorial assistance. The information provided on some locomotive data is from *Diesel Locomotive Rosters* published by Wayner Publications, 1973. Thanks to friends who refreshed my memory with facts and general information: Alex Bruchac, Al Bush, Allen Clum, Blaine Hays, Sheldon Lustig, Jim McMullen, Dr. Craig Sanders, Bill Surdyk, and John Swift. Any errors in the text are my responsibility.

Finally, to old friends Bill Brodie and Russ Lynch, who have said for years "Gee, I wish you would do a book. I'd buy it": *Well guys, here it is: enjoy!*

Dave McKay

TABLE OF CONTENTS

PREVIOUS PAGE • A westbound freight crossed the Cuyahoga River Valley on September 24, 1978. The name "Cuyahoga" means "crooked river" and this shot shows how the river bends and twists through Cleveland on its way to Lake Erie. It was a challenge for the big lake boats to navigate their way to the industries and docks along the river, although improvements to the waterway over many years allowed lake boats of up to 600 feet in length to operate. This picture was taken on September 24, 1978 when the curb lane of the I-90 interbelt bridge was closed for repairs, enabling the shot to be taken safely.

DAVE McKAY

TRACKSIDE *Photographer*

I was born in Youngstown, Ohio in August of 1943. When I was an infant, my family moved to East Cleveland, Ohio. The main line of the Nickel Plate Road was 900 feet from my bedroom window. I've always believed that if you grow up next to the tracks, you either love trains all your life or hate them. Since there were no railroaders in my family history, I guess I got hooked. There were wonderful memories of the NKP's 2-8-4s and PAs, and the sounds of an Alco S2 switching Keiner Coal Company on a warm evening.

Many Sunday afternoons were spent at the Worden Road grade crossing in Wickliffe, Ohio. The New York Central and Nickel Plate paralleled one another from there to Willoughby. Mother picked elderberries along the New York Central, and after the EMPIRE STATE EXPRESS passed, we would call it a day. But it was the NKP Berkshires on fast freights that I remember best of all.

The family moved again, to South Euclid, in 1950. I lobbied for trackside in Wickliffe or Willoughby, but when you are only seven years old, you move where the folks decide to go! Away from the tracks, my interest in trains went to limbo. But in the summer of 1959, Father announced that we were going on a three-week trip out west, to visit as many national parks as we could. Dad's boss suggested getting a 35mm camera for the trip. Dad took me down to Reitman Camera, as I was designated the trip photographer. Irv Math sold us a Beauty Super L camera. It was a rangefinder style camera with a 45mm f1.9 lens, and shutter speeds up to 1/500th a second. A test roll resulted in, first, a shot of our house; second, an action shot of a Nickel Plate RS11 on the Conneaut local. All of a sudden, trains weren't speed-blurred. Wow! As a result, I stayed shooting slides and never looked back. That western trip gave me my first taste of the Union Pacific, the Denver & Rio Grande Western, and Santa Fe red and silver.

That experience started an interest in railroads and photography that has never waned. I attended Rochester Institute of Technology in Rochester, New York from 1961 to 1965. I received a B. S. degree in Professional Photography that has led to a career in the photo-finishing business. I still have the old Beauty Super L, but changed to Nikons beginning in 1967. A Kodachrome II/25 user for many years, I have currently settled on using Fuji Provia 100F film.

I started railfanning on a grand scale after graduation from R. I. T. in 1965. The Cleveland area found all five of the big Eastern roads present: New York Central and Nickel Plate, Baltimore & Ohio, Erie Lackawanna, and Pennsylvania. Frequent trips to Youngstown, to visit relatives, resulted in a good deal of coverage of the rail scene in that area. In this volume, we will take a look at my favorite slides from Cleveland and other locations within a 75-mile radius of the city. Before we begin our illustrated tour, however, let's examine the Cleveland area and the railroads that helped make it one of America's great industrial and transportation centers.

Here I am in the cab of a B&O SW900 switcher in the Lincoln Park roundhouse at Rochester, New York in March 1962.

I'm up in the cab of a Santa Fe PA1 at Summit, Illinois on April 6, 1969. ATSF PA and PB units were stored on a siding off the Indiana Harbor Belt awaiting scrapping at Pielet Brothers.

TRACKSIDE *around* CLEVELAND 1965-1979 *with* Dave McKay

CLEVELAND AND NORTHEASTERN OHIO

Cleveland rose to prominence in the 19th century, as its location on Lake Erie at the mouth of the curving Cuyahoga River made it an ideal location for heavy industry and transportation. At the end of the 18th century, the Connecticut Land Company acquired a sizeable tract of land, called the Western Reserve, along the shore of Lake Erie. General Anthony Wayne's victories over the Indians had made white settlements possible, and the company sent a Connecticut native, General Moses Cleaveland (more in a bit on the spelling of the name) to survey the property, which stretched for 120 miles along the lake shore. The mouth of the Cuyahoga River was at the midpoint of the holdings, and it was here that Cleaveland laid out plans for a major settlement. Not much happened at first, but the town's growth in the early 1800s was based on waterborne commerce: steamboats that began to operate on the Great Lakes, and then the impact of canals. The Erie Canal through New York State opened in 1825 and provided a way for commerce to move easily from the East Coast to the Midwest. Ohio caught the canal fever, and built the Ohio and Erie Canal to connect Lake Erie at Cleveland with the Ohio River. By 1832, the canal was operating all the way to the Ohio, and the city began to grow rapidly, as it continued to do for most of the century.

More change was to come at mid-century. The Soo Canal, linking Lake Superior with the lower Great Lakes, opened in 1855 and allowed copper and iron ore to move by water to lake ports like Cleveland. Railroads came to Cleveland beginning in the 1830s, and by the 1850s linked the city to the east, west, and south. The discovery of oil in western Pennsylvania at roughly the same time allowed petroleum to move to Cleveland, which John D. Rockefeller made his home and the home of his industry-leading Standard Oil Company. Coal from Appalachia came north by rail and met iron ore from Michigan and Minnesota coming by water, and Cleveland was a logical place for a major steel industry to grow and flourish, as it did also along the Mahoning Valley and Youngstown. Close to the major markets in the Northeast and Midwest, with excellent raw materials and transportation facilities, Cleveland grew until it became the sixth largest city in the nation, with almost a million residents and the anchor of a major urban region that fanned out from the city on the lake. Cleveland was a classic American city of the industrial era, with well-defined neighborhoods home to a variety of ethnic groups, and a pall of smoke from the industries and railroads a reminder of the industrial basis of its economy.

About that spelling: for the July 1, 1832 masthead of a new paper, the printer had to drop one letter to fit the available space, and rather than shorten the paper's impressive name, *The Cleveland Gazette and Commercial Register*, dropped the "a" from the previous name. General Cleaveland was long gone from the scene, and apparently no one else felt it necessary to complain, so "Cleveland" it came to be known from then on.

RAILROADS OF CLEVELAND

Bustling Cleveland was too valuable a location for any railroad to pass by if it could find a way in. They found a city roughly divided into east and west by the curving valley of the Cuyahoga. The commercial and residential sections of Cleveland are mostly on high ground above the river valley, which became the home of heavy industry and called by all Clevelanders simply "The Flats." The New York Central and Nickel Plate wound their way through the city as a natural result of following the lake shore on their east/west main lines, while the other three roads extended lines from their East Coast/Chicago mains to reach Cleveland and the lake. We'll look at each of the major roads and some of the industrial, electric traction, and regional and short line roads that made the Cleveland area one of the most interesting rail centers in the country.

The New York Central had the greatest presence in Cleveland. There were three different routes through Cleveland from BE Tower at Berea on the southwest side of the city to QD (called "Quaker" by Conrail) at the west end of Collinwood Yard on the northeast side of Cleveland. The *Lakefront Line* operated between BE and QD passing near Cleveland Hopkins International Airport, West Park, Whiskey Island, DB drawbridge at the mouth of the Cuyahoga River, Cleveland Municipal Stadium, and the Village of Bratenahl. The second line was the *Cleveland Union Terminal (CUT)* passenger line. The CUT operated on the former Big Four trackage from Linndale to Fulton Road, then on its own line through Cleveland Union Terminal and parallel to the Nickel Plate main line from E. 38th Street to East Cleveland. At East Cleveland the CUT turned to the northeast along Hayden Avenue to QD at Collinwood. The third line was called *The Short Line*. The Short Line started at CP 190 on the Lakefront Line, entered Rockport Yard, and ran east along the Cleveland/Parma border, crossing the Cuyahoga River Valley on the Marcy Trestle. Marcy Interlocking at the east end of the trestle is where the Lake Erie & Pittsburgh line headed south to reach the coal fields of southern Ohio. At Marcy, the Short Line turned northeast and led through the near-eastside Cleveland neighborhoods until it joined the CUT line at Fairhill Road, paralleling the CUT to QD. The Short Line was built between 1910 and 1912 and served as a freight bypass around the congested downtown area.

Berea was the junction of the Central's east/west, former Lake Shore & Michigan Southern main with the former Big Four mainline to Columbus, Cincinnati and St. Louis. A fourth line into the city, the Big Four line ran from BE to Linndale and then on joint trackage with the CUT to Fulton Road. At Fulton Road, the Big Four diverged from the CUT and wound its way down the Cuyahoga River valley to a wye connection with the Lakefront Line at the east end of DB.

Cleveland became not just a major center of freight activity on the Central, but also a major passenger center, with the NYC offering trains that conveniently linked Cleveland with almost all the major cities of the East and Midwest: Chicago, Detroit, Cincinnati, Buffalo, St. Louis, New York, and Boston. Until the end of name passenger trains on the NYC in the 1960s, it proudly carried such train names as 20TH CENTURY LIMITED, OHIO STATE EXPRESS, EMPIRE STATE EXPRESS, and COMMODORE VANDERBILT into Cleveland's impressive Union Terminal.

The Nickel Plate Road – officially the New York, Chicago, & St. Louis – traversed the heart of Cleveland on its Chicago-Buffalo main line. From the west, the NKP entered the city via Rocky River and Lakewood. Crossing the Cuyahoga Valley on a long trestle with a vertical lift bridge, the line continued eastward with a large yard located at East 55th Street, and a small engine facility at East 75th Street. It paralleled the CUT line to East Cleveland and continued east through Euclid, Wickliffe, Willoughby and Painesville on its way to Erie and Buffalo. At Painesville's PE Tower, the NKP main line crossed the Baltimore & Ohio's Fairport Branch from Niles, Ohio, one of the many lines in the region designed mostly to move coal to Lake Erie.

Besides the original Nickel Plate line described above, the NKP also operated the former Wheeling & Lake Erie line that entered Cleveland from the southeast. The NKP leased the W&LE in 1948; both lines had formerly been part of the collection of railroads put together by two of Cleveland's most prominent entrepreneurs, the Van Sweringen brothers. The Wheeling line entered Cleveland from the southeast and terminated at Campbell Road Yard in The Flats. The Wheeling also had trackage rights on the Big Four from Wellington to Ridge Road in Cleveland, with an entrance to Campbell Road Yard from the west. The W&LE operated an 8-mile branch from Falls Junction to Solon and Chagrin Falls.

In October of 1964, the Nickel Plate was merged into the growing Norfolk & Western, which also gained control of the Akron, Canton, and Youngstown. Most of the shots in this volume on the former NKP and W&LE lines are from the N&W period.

The Pennsylvania Railroad reached Cleveland over its C&P (Cleveland & Pittsburgh) line, which joined the PRR's Pittsburgh-Chicago main line at Alliance, Ohio, 83 miles west of Pittsburgh. The C&P terminated on Whiskey Island, the site of a large iron ore unloading facility. The PRR had trackage rights at DB over the New York Central to access the island. The ore moved down the C&P to the mills of the Ohio River Valley, at locations such as Weirton, West Virginia and Steubenville, Ohio. One of the prime attractions of the PRR's Whiskey Island operations in the busy summer months was the quartet of Hulett unloaders used to empty the lake boats; another was the fleet of blue and gray GP7s it leased from the Bangor & Aroostook to switch the ore docks.

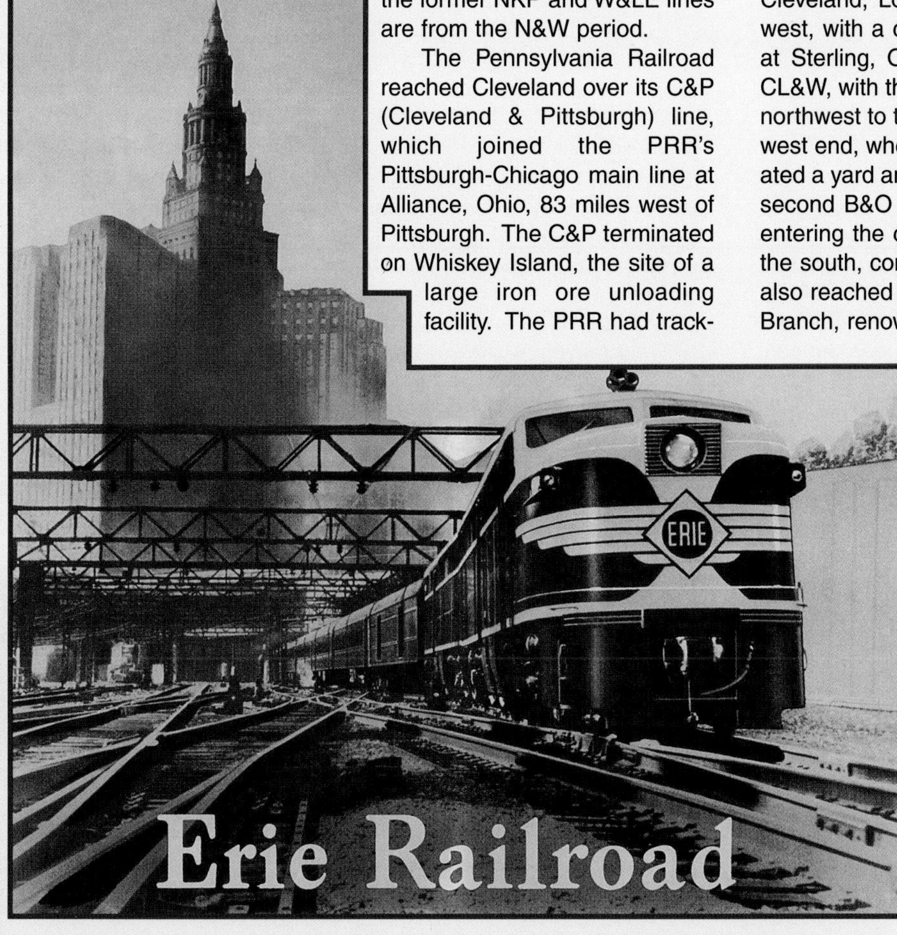

The Erie Lackawanna entered Cleveland on a line that branched off its former Erie Railroad New Jersey-Chicago main at Leavittsburg, Ohio. Like the PRR, the EL used Cleveland harbor as a loading area for iron ore that moved down its line to the mills of Youngstown and the Mahoning Valley. The EL operated its own ore dock along the Cuyahoga River. A yard at East 55th Street handled general freight and featured an engine terminal for its motive power. The Nickel Plate, the Erie's former Van Sweringen ally, used the turntable at the EL's facility to turn power if needed. The EL serviced most of the Cleveland area food markets in North Randall, Bedford Heights, and Solon. Although it didn't have the greatest impact on Cleveland railroading, the EL provided a great show as Cleveland to Youngstown ore trains struggled up the grade out of the river bed from the ore docks to North Randall; as we'll see, the EL assigned its heaviest diesel power, Train Masters and later U33Cs, for this tough work. The EL also operated passenger trains on the Cleveland-Youngstown run, becoming the final passenger operator using Cleveland Union Terminal until commuter train #28 made its final run on January 14, 1977. In the otherwise drab world of Cleveland railroading, with somber dark solid color schemes the rule for most diesel locomotives, the bright EL engines also provided an injection of color that made its operations photogenic.

The fifth of the major eastern lines serving Cleveland was the Baltimore & Ohio. The B&O had two lines into Cleveland. The Cleveland, Lorain & Wheeling line (CL&W) entered from the southwest, with a connection with the B&O's Pittsburgh-Chicago main line at Sterling, Ohio. The Cleveland line was one of two lines of the CL&W, with the other leaving the Cleveland line at Lester and heading northwest to the lake at Lorain. The Cleveland line terminated at DB's west end, where it met the New York Central's Lakefront Line. It operated a yard and an engine facility at West 3rd Street in Cleveland. The second B&O line into Cleveland also terminated at West 3rd Street, entering the city along the scenic valley of the Cuyahoga River from the south, connecting with the main line at Akron Junction. The B&O also reached the northeast Ohio region from the south on its Fairport Branch, renowned for its use of EM1 2-8-8-4s late in their career and a favorite of such noted photographers as Jim Shaughhnessy and Philip Hastings.

REGIONALS, SHORTLINES, AND INDUSTRIALS

Although the official designation of "regional" railroad is fairly recent, two railroads in the Cleveland area fit that description, too long and busy to be called shortlines but too limited to compare with the five major carriers in the area. One was the 169.3 mile Akron, Canton & Youngstown, which operated across the state of Ohio from Mogadore in the east, east of Akron, to Delphos. Akron was the center of AC&Y operations, with the road's headquarters and main shops. Its operations centered on Brittain Yard, off Market Street on the east side of the Tire City. The AC&Y operated in an east/west direction, and did not extend to the Cleveland urban area. Its claim to fame in the diesel era was its fleet of yellow Fairbanks-Morse road switchers, augmented by a smaller number of Alco units.

While the AC&Y was strictly an Ohio operation, the second regional railroad in the northeast Ohio region was primarily a Pennsylvania road, the Bessemer & Lake Erie. The B&LE operated 152.9 miles from its southern terminus, at North Bessemer, Pennsylvania outside Pittsburgh, to Lake Erie, which it reached at Erie, Pennsylvania and Conneaut, Ohio. The main line extended north from North Bessemer to Albion, Pennsylvania, where the 12.8 Conneaut Branch left the main line to Erie at NA Tower at the north end of Albion Yard. The large dock operation at Conneaut was operated by the Pittsburgh & Conneaut Dock Company. Iron ore was loaded at Conneaut for the U. S. Steel mills around Pittsburgh; the B&LE was part of the U. S. Steel family of railroads primarily owned to service the steel industry. The B&LE was a conduit for ore moving south and bituminous coal moving north, to be transloaded to lake boats at Conneaut and Erie. Like the AC&Y, the Bessemer's fleet of orange engines was a major attraction for railfans, beginning with its large fleet of F7s and including such rare types as Alco RSD15s and EMD SD18s.

The region also was home to several interesting shortlines. The *Fairport, Painesville & Eastern* was a switching and terminal road that primarily served the Diamond Shamrock Chemical Company complex at Fairport Harbor, on Lake Erie east of Cleveland. It interchanged with the New York Central and Nickel Plate at Perry, Ohio and the B&O at Fairport Harbor. It was merged into the N&W in 1984.

The *Youngstown & Southern* began as an interurban line and was later dieselized. It leased two SW7s from the Montour Railroad in western Pennsylvania. Most of the Y&S's business was in Youngstown and Boardman, Ohio; it interchanged with the PRR and P&LE at Struthers, Ohio.

As might be expected in a major industrial center like Cleveland, a number of industrial railroads also enlivened the railroad scene. Cleveland had three major steel mill complexes, and each operated its own railroad. Jones & Laughlin Steel operated the *Cuyahoga Valley Railroad* at its mill complex. Republic Steel had its own engines as well as those of its common carrier affiliate, *River Terminal Railway*. The U. S. Steel Company operated the *Newburgh & South Shore*, serving two USS operations, the Cuyahoga Works on East 49th Street and the American Steel & Wire mill along the Cuyahoga in The Flats.

Two major electric power companies entered the railroad scene in the 1970s, with their own fleet of locomotives and unit trains of hopper cars operating through the Cleveland area. The *Cleveland Electric Illuminating Company (CEI)* had a fleet of blue and yellow GP38-2s. The *Detroit Edison Company* operated blue and silver SD40s and U30Cs that passed through the region on the route between the coal fields in Greene County, Pennsylvania on the Monongahela Railroad and the DE's power plant at Monroe, Michigan.

ELECTRIC TRACTION

Cleveland was an early center of the electrical industry. Under the inventive Charles F. Brush, Cleveland was one of the first big cities to be lighted by electric lights in the 1880s, and Brush built a thriving electrics company manufacturing batteries and generators in the city. Electric street railways began operating in Cleveland in 1884, and were run by such eminent figures as Mark Hanna, industrialist and U. S. Senator, and the reform mayor Thomas Lofton Johnson. Later, the entrepreneurial brothers, Oris P. and Mantis J. Van Sweringen, combined interests in electric railways, real estate development, and steam railways to extend electric transit from the new suburb of Shaker Heights. From the 1940s until the formation of a regional transit authority in 1974, the remaining lines of the Van Sweringen's Cleveland Interurban Railway continued to link downtown and Shaker Heights on two lines. The major line ran from Cleveland Union Terminal to Shaker Square. The Green Road line followed the median of Shaker Boulevard to Green Road. The second line branched off the Green Road line at Van Aken Boulevard and terminated on Van Aken at Warrensville Center Road and Chagrin Boulevard. The line was run with PCC cars until replaced in the late 1970s with LRV cars built in Italy.

A second rapid transit system was opened in 1955. The Cleveland Transit System ran from Windermere Station in East Cleveland to West Park (Lorain Avenue). The Rapid followed the NKP and CUT lines on the east side of the city, and the NKP and Lakefront Line of the NYC on the west side. Between Cleveland Union Terminal and East 55th Street the CTS and the Shaker Rapid shared joint trackage. CTS used cars built by St. Louis Car Company in 1954. In 1968 the Rapid was extended to Cleveland Hopkins International Airport from West Park, making Cleveland one of the first cities to have its airport connected to downtown by rapid transit.

On December 30, 1974 The Greater Cleveland Regional Transit Authority – called the RTA – was created to run public transportation in Cuyahoga County. RTA also assumed control of the Shaker Heights Rapid Transit. The Shaker Rapid had been owned and operated by the city of Shaker Heights since 1944. A referendum on a sales tax increased to subsidize operations of the system was approved by voters on July 22, 1975. The RTA modernized equipment and coordinated services within the expanded system.

Summing up, Cleveland and the surrounding northeast Ohio region had a variety of railroads and rail operations that covered the gamut from main lines to branch lines to urban freight and rapid transit lines. The importance of the steel industry and Cleveland's location on Lake Erie influenced much of what moved on the rails around Cleveland. In this volume, we'll cover all these roads as we provide a sense of what railroading in Cleveland was like from the 1960s up to more recent years. We begin with a look at the major railroads, moving then to the shorter lines and traction, and including a glimpse of some of the steam specials that livened things up on occasion. Railroading around Cleveland had its ups and downs in the years after I began shooting in the 1960s, with Penn Central and then Conrail replacing the New York Central, Pennsylvania, and Erie Lackawanna, and the B&O swallowed up by the Chessie System and then CSX. But there was always variety and lots of action on the railroads of Cleveland, as I hope this book shows.

I posed for the camera at Highland Cut on the former Pennsylvania Railroad in Pennsylvania on September 11, 1998.

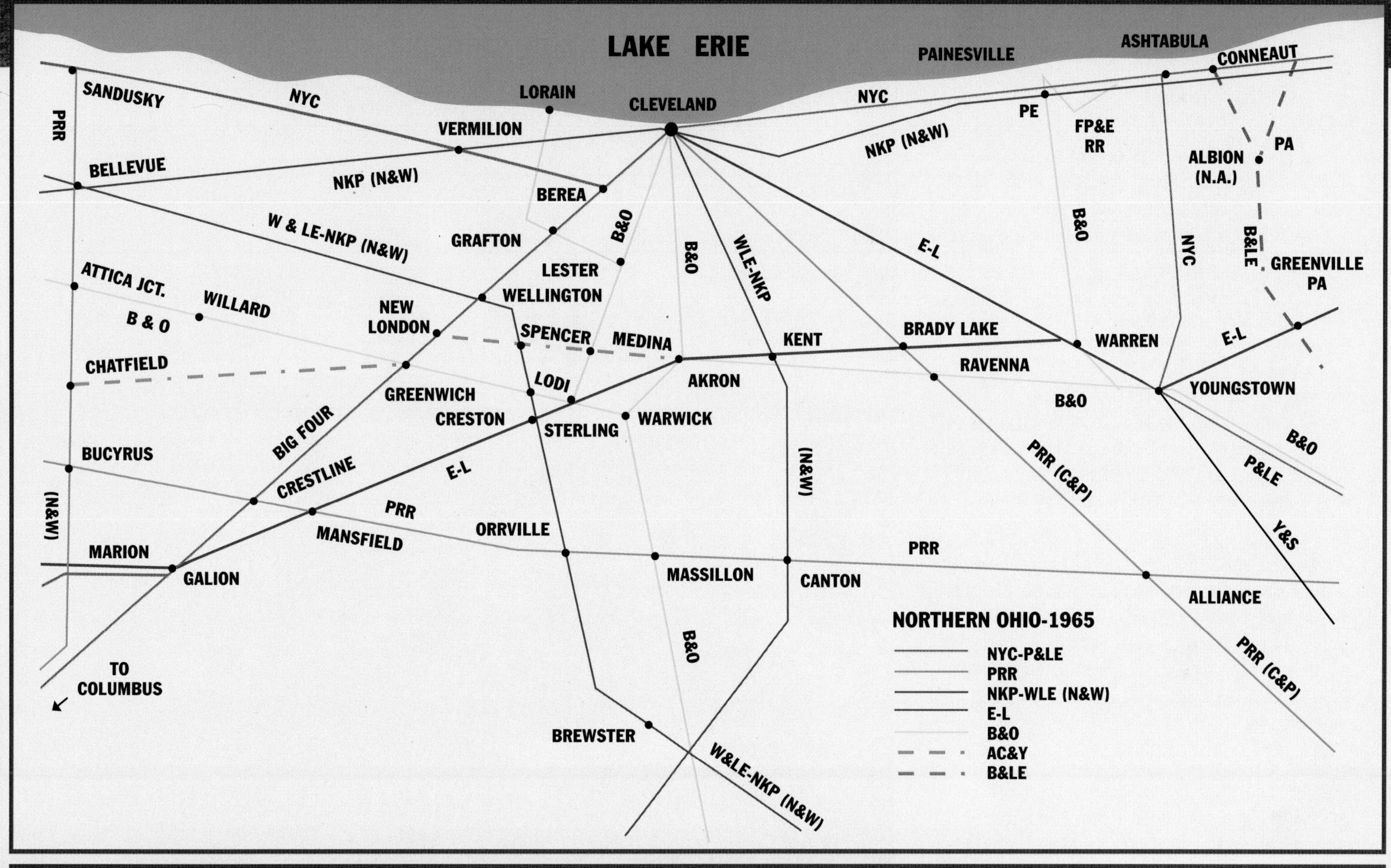
LAKE ERIE
NORTHERN OHIO-1965
NYC-P&LE
PRR
NKP-WLE (N&W)
E-L
B&O
AC&Y
B&LE
SANDUSKY
BELLEVUE
LORAIN
VERMILION
CLEVELAND
PAINESVILLE
ASHTABULA
CONNEAUT
ALBION (N.A.)
PA
GREENVILLE PA
BEREA
GRAFTON
LESTER
WELLINGTON
ATTICA JCT.
WILLARD
NEW LONDON
SPENCER
MEDINA
KENT
BRADY LAKE
WARREN
RAVENNA
YOUNGSTOWN
CHATFIELD
GREENWICH
LODI
AKRON
CRESTON
STERLING
WARWICK
BUCYRUS
CRESTLINE
MANSFIELD
ORRVILLE
MARION
GALION
MASSILLON
CANTON
ALLIANCE
BREWSTER
TO COLUMBUS
W & LE-NKP (N&W)
W&LE-NKP (N&W)
WLE-NKP
BIG FOUR
FP&E RR
PE
P&LE
Y&S

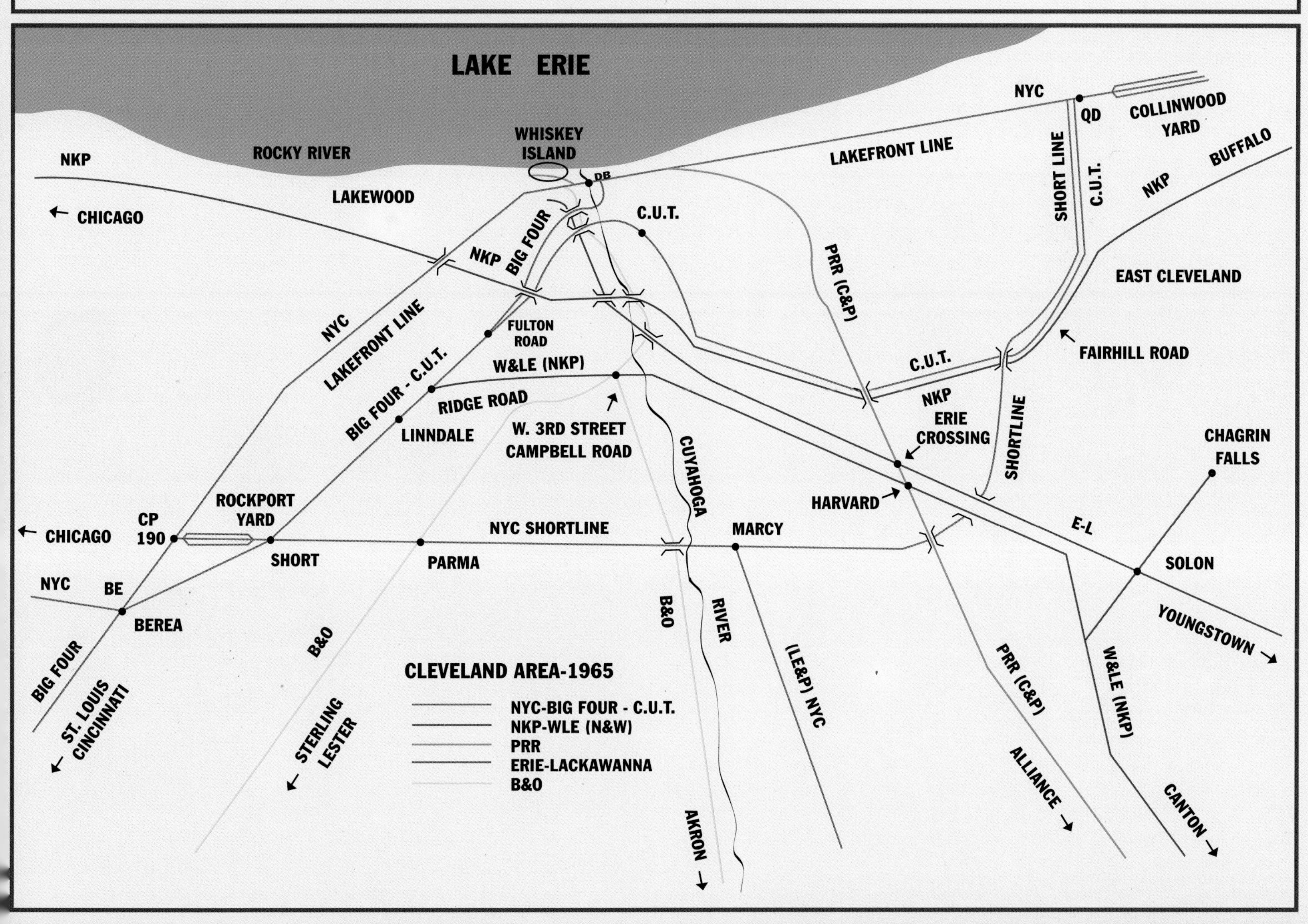
LAKE ERIE
CLEVELAND AREA-1965
NYC-BIG FOUR - C.U.T.
NKP-WLE (N&W)
PRR
ERIE-LACKAWANNA
B&O
ROCKY RIVER
WHISKEY ISLAND
DB
LAKEWOOD
CHICAGO
C.U.T.
LAKEFRONT LINE
SHORT LINE
QD
COLLINWOOD YARD
BUFFALO
EAST CLEVELAND
FULTON ROAD
W&LE (NKP)
RIDGE ROAD
LINNDALE
W. 3RD STREET CAMPBELL ROAD
CUYAHOGA RIVER
PRR (C&P)
FAIRHILL ROAD
NKP ERIE CROSSING
HARVARD
SHORTLINE
CHAGRIN FALLS
ROCKPORT YARD
CP 190
SHORT
PARMA
NYC SHORTLINE
MARCY
SOLON
BE
BEREA
YOUNGSTOWN
ST. LOUIS CINCINNATI
STERLING LESTER
AKRON
(LE&P) NYC
ALLIANCE
CANTON

Collinwood

(Right) Freight operations on the New York Central around Cleveland centered on the large yard and shops at Collinwood, on the east side of Cleveland. Collinwood Yard and shops dated back to 1874, with significant expansion in 1903 and 1929. With the arrival of the Cleveland Union Terminal P-1a electric motors after CUT was opened, a five-track shop was built for them between East 152nd Street and QD Tower in the southwest corner of Collinwood Yard. In July 1968, at the end of the New York Central era and the beginning of Penn Central, it's all still NYC as FA2 1382 and GP35 2380 share the facility with an assortment of Geeps and SW 8606.

(Right) Around 1961, a modern fuel and service facility was constructed adjacent to the electric motor shop complex. FA2 1045 and FBs 3330 and 3324 rest between calls in November 1967. All three of the Alcos were built in 1951, and were part of the Central's large fleet of Alco freight cabs.

(Below) The East 152nd Street overpass was an excellent vantage point from which to photograph all the yard activity at Collinwood. Collinwood is about seven miles northeast of central Cleveland. It was once a separate village but was annexed by the city of Cleveland in 1910. FA2 1122 led a westbound out of the yard ahead of three other FAs on March 22, 1964.

(Above) At Dille Road, on the east side of Collinwood Yard, the NYC had a main-line refueling facility. In November 1965, eastbound auto-rack train ML-12 had three EMD units added to its consist of four U25Bs for a fast trip east. ML-12's symbol indicated "multi-level", the Central's acronym for auto trains. ML-12 originated in Detroit and was bound for Selkirk Yard outside Albany, New York, with New England connections over the Boston & Albany line of the NYC. Lead unit 6127 was part of the Central's first order for GP35s in December 1963.

(Below) Extra units were commonly added to eastbound trains at Dille Road. On this day in May 1966, NY-4 received two FA2s, 1098 and 1060, to assist a trio of EMDs. The Central purchased 80 FA2s and 50 FB2s in 1951/52, adding to the already sizeable roster of 44 FA1s and 23 FB1s it had acquired in 1947/48. By the last years of the NYC before the Penn Central merger, their numbers were thinning as newer EMD and GE power replaced the cab units.

Collinwood Shops

(Right) The General Office building for the Collinwood Shops was at 577 East 152nd Street. This is how it looked on July 9, 1972. The shops were closed by Conrail in 1981, resulting in the layoff of 250 workers.

(Above) The Collinwood Shops performed heavy repairs on all types of diesels. The service tracks by the paint shop along East 152nd Street always had good light in the afternoon to shoot the engines worked on at Collinwood. Baldwin DRS4-4-1500 7300 was shot there on July 18, 1964. Equipped with steam generators, the 7300 and sister unit 7301 were originally numbered 8300/8301. They were re-engined at Collinwood with EMD 567 prime movers in 1956 and were based at Englewood, Illinois and often used to switch LaSalle Street Station in Chicago. The unit was built in 1948 and retired in 1966.

QD Tower

(Left) Let's move to the west side of Collinwood and take a look at the action around QD Tower. On April 25, 1967 train SV-9 departed Collinwood at QD with GP35 2394 ahead of the three Alco Century 430 demonstrators in their attractive gray, red and white color scheme. The C430s barnstormed around the country on several railroads and were seen by Alco as a competitor for EMD's popular GP40 and GE's U30B, also 3,000 horsepower B-B units. The Central was apparently impressed and ordered 10 of the units, its last purchase from Alco, which arrived in December 1967. My thanks to QD operator Tom Robinson for the phone call that tipped me off to this unusual movement.

(Above) A westbound was leaving Collinwood at QD in December 1967 with Missouri Pacific GP18 418 in the consist, riding on trade-in Alco trucks. Note the differences in the "cigar band" lettering and numbering schemes between the first and third F7s and the middle unit.

(Left) An eastbound hot slab train was coming off the Short Line at QD interlocking on February 24, 1968. The tracks under the Short Line bridge are those of the Lakefront main line to downtown and Berea. The brick building behind the last unit and first cars is the old G. C. Kuhlman Car Company. The Kuhlman Company built many streetcars during the heyday of electric traction. Cleveland Rapid Transit line car 024 and former Shaker Rapid car 12 survive today as Kuhlman Company alumni.

Passenger Action at Collinwood

(Right) I was standing on the top step of QD Tower in November 1965 to get this shot of westbound train #59, THE CHICAGOAN, as it passed through Collinwood on its way to Cleveland Union Terminal and points west. A pair of E8s in the cigar band scheme was the power for the Chicago-bound train.

(Left) On January 20, 1968 I was at track level to record #59 as it paused at Collinwood for a crew change and servicing. This train always carried a healthy cut of head-end cars.

(Below) At the site of the former passenger station in East Cleveland, westbound #59 rounded the curve and passed alongside the Nickel Plate's main line tracks to Buffalo in August 1966.

East of Collinwood

(Above) Heading west through Mentor, Ohio this freight had F7A 1756 leading, nearing the grade crossing of Route 306 in March 1962. Today this once-rural area between Painesville and Willoughby has been transformed into strip malls and fast food restaurants as the metropolis expands eastward. Mentor, founded in 1799, was once a quiet Western Reserve town noted as the home of one of Ohio's many 19th century presidents, James A. Garfield.

(Below) FA2 1049 led this smoky all-Alco consist west at Conneaut, Ohio on May 15, 1966. In the 1960s it was fairly routine to find RS3s and Alco cabs working together, as the Central began to use 5 or 6 of the older units on freights. The Central owned 135 RS3s and used them in all kinds of service, from main line freights like this to locals and suburban passenger trains.

(Right) A quartet of U25Bs had ML-12 rolling its consist of new autos eastward at the Ohio Route 44 overpass at Painesville, Ohio on August 8, 1965. Not too long after crossing the Ohio/Pennsylvania border they will pass near their place of birth at GE's Erie locomotive works. The New York Central was an enthusiastic purchaser of U25Bs, adding 70 of the type to the roster in 1964/65 as part of the transformation from first to second generation diesel power.

(Inset) An unusual set of power was moving this westbound freight through Erie, Pennsylvania on February 20, 1966. Alco RS11 8008 led three P&LE GP7s through the Erie passenger station. The lead unit was the last of an order of nine RS11s, 8000-8008, built by Alco in 1957.

8008
NEW YORK CENTRAL SYSTEM
NEW YORK CENTRAL
2559
2533
NEW YORK CENTRAL
NEW YORK CENTRAL
2524 2524
2524
CENTRAL

(Right) On the west side of Cleveland, FA2 1065 and two RS3s were working hard to move this freight west at the West 150th Street grade crossing on February 12, 1966. After the extension of the Rapid Transit from West Park to Hopkins Airport in 1968 the grade crossing was replaced with an overpass.

Berea

(Right) Berea was the hotspot on the west side of town. The Lakefront, CUT and Short Line tracks joined at the east side of Berea, and just to the west the Toledo Division main line to Toledo and Chicago diverged from the Big Four main. On April 16, 1966 westbound train #59 was crossing over to the Toledo Division main after coming over the CUT line, on its way to the Windy City.

(Above) BE Tower at Berea controlled the movements through this hotspot. On April 16, 1966 a westbound freight on the Lakefront main line swung by BE with four Alco cab units in charge; the tower is out of sight behind me as the train rounds the gentle curve east of the junction with the Short Line.

(Left) The NYC purchased 105 of EMD's 3,000 horsepower GP40s in 1966/67 as it settled on high-horsepower B-B road switchers for its modern freight power. On this day, August 3, 1969, GP40 3022 had an unusual partner moving this west-bound freight: Alco C636 demonstrator 636-1. The train is now working for Penn Central, and the C636 is the final bid for ailing Alco to stay in the diesel locomotive business. You would not have seen the NYC, which was committed to four-axle power, buying such a locomotive, but PC purchased fifteen. As we will see, they found their way to Cleveland, usually not on trains like this through Berea, but more often on the ore trains using former PRR trackage from the docks to the steel mills. BE Tower is clearly visible as the train rounds the curve on the Lakefront Line; the Short Line tracks are just to my rear and out of sight.

Night Time at Berea

(Right) On the evening of August 15, 1962 I experimented with night action shots at BE Tower. Using High-Speed Ektachrome film at ASA 160 and one #5B flashbulb, I was able to freeze an eastbound freight moving past the tower led by Fairbanks-Morse CFA16-4 6600 from the tower window. The flash was able to stop the action and also catch a rare well-lit glimpse into the cab of the engine, with both engineer and fireman clearly visible.

(Below) I was able to shoot not only the head end of the train, but also this classic wooden New York Central caboose at the rear end. The crewman in the caboose is exchanging lantern signals with the tower operator in BE, and is adorned in traditional railroad style: soft white cap and denim jacket.

On the Fringes

(Left) Outside the immediate Cleveland area but still within the 75-mile radius were many photogenic locations on the New York Central. At New London, Ohio, on the Big Four, the Central crossed the Akron, Canton & Youngstown main at grade at Hiles Tower. On May 21, 1967 three F7s moved westbound freight over the AC&Y and past the tower west of Cleveland.

(Above) On the other side of the region, a northbound train was leaving the Pittsburgh & Lake Erie's Gateway Yard in Struthers, Ohio on its way to Ashtabula, Ohio on February 18, 1968. I was standing on the Bridge Street overpass to get this shot. F7 1701 led a pair of leased B&LE units as the train passed the hump at Gateway on its way to the docks at Lake Erie.

(Left) Cleveland's grandest and most famous building, the Terminal Tower Building at the southwest corner of Public Square, rose 52 stories and 708' above the Cleveland Union Terminal railroad station. Completed in 1927, the Tower housed offices of the Van Sweringen railroads, and was part of a complex of buildings including a hotel, a department store, smaller office buildings, and a post office. Its unusual design, by the Chicago firm of Graham, Anderson, Probst & White, topped by the complex turreted tower itself, made it an instant landmark, even as the fortunes of the Van Sweringens quickly crumbled in the Great Depression. I shot this view of the Terminal Tower from The Mall on July 4, 1980, after the building had been restored for the 50th anniversary of the celebration of the opening of the termnal group on June 29, 1930. The first train actually entered the terminal some months before, on October 23, 1929, a month after the Stock Market crash that was to change the fortunes of its builders profoundly.

(Above) Here is a view of the restored portico of the Tower at the main entrance. The view is looking toward the *Hotel Cleveland*, and was taken September 14, 1980.

(Right) A view of the main waiting room of CUT with track gates shows one of the murals adorning the walls, taken on May 3, 1969. No expense was spared when the grand edifice was built, at the end of the Roaring Twenties when travel by rail was still the foundation of the nation's transportation system. The terminal and buildings built on air rights above it covered 17 acres. The offices of the Cleveland Union Terminal are behind the mural. CUT hosted from its inception trains of the New York Central, Nickel Plate, and B&O, and later saw trains of Erie Lackawanna also operating from its tracks. The Shaker Heights Rapid Transit system used the terminal as its downtown terminus beginning in 1930, as did the Cleveland Transit System and RTA in more recent times. The only major player in the Cleveland rail scene that never used CUT was the Pennsylvania Railroad.

CT Tower

(Left) CT Tower controlled all of the tracks and signals of Cleveland Union Terminal between East 34th Street and West 25th Street in the city. Wally Safner is at the tower director's desk on the evening of December 17, 1966.

(Left) There was nothing small about Cleveland Union Terminal! On December 17, 1966 operator Wally Safner made a line-up at CT Tower. When CUT opened in 1930, this was the largest GRS electro-mechanical interlocking machine in the country, with 576 levers.

(Left) By the time I returned to CT Tower in January 1968, fluorescent lighting had been installed to replace the incandescent lighting in place for my 1966 shots. Railfan Jim McMullen was testing out a couple of the levers under the guidance of Wally Safner. Unlike some smaller towers, CT was clean and well-maintained in the 1960s.

Train Time at Cleveland Union Terminal

(Above) September 9, 1961 was the date of the final run of train #323. It is seen heading west over the Cuyahoga Valley Viaduct on its way to Cincinnati, with Chesapeake & Ohio Pullman car *City of Pikeville* bringing up the rear. A pall of industrial haze covers the city, par for the course in the late summer in Cleveland in the days when the steel mills were still working at full capacity.

(Below) On May 6, 1961 an A/B set of lightning-striped E7s prepared to lead the westbound CHICAGOAN out of CUT on the way west to Chicago. The Central purchased 50 E7s, 36 A units and 16 B units, helping to make the model EMD's best-selling passenger diesel.

(All) In a series of views taken in November 1967, train #59 emerges from the depths of CUT and heads west over the viaduct. The first shot conveys the enormity of the Terminal Tower building and complex. The lead unit, E7A 4014, wears a fresh coat of gray just months before the Penn Central merger. Was this the last New York Central passenger unit to get new paint before the merger? Perhaps a New York Central expert can answer this one. 4014 has the large angled number boards that all but the earliest NYC E7s used.

(Above) Penn Central renumbered train #59 to #63 after the merger. The train left New York City's Grand Central Station at 10:30 PM and arrived five minutes after noon at CUT, where it was scheduled for 55 minutes before leaving at 1 PM, the time required to work the heavy head-end business carried by the train. In a scene that shows the relationship of CUT to the network of tracks along the Cuyahoga, we see #63 heading out of the terminal on February 7, 1970. Directly above the lead unit is the Victorian era yellow-brick building that housed the B&O's Cleveland offices and at one time served as the road's passenger station. Diamond Jim's restaurant seen in the lower left of the photo occupies the former passenger station of the Erie Railroad that was accessed on trackage rights over the Big Four. Rising above it all is the magnificent Terminal Tower.

(Right) Leaving the New York Central, let's examine the operations around Cleveland of its bitter competitor and eventual merger partner, the Pennsylvania Railroad. For the PRR, Cleveland was first and foremost a lake port location useful for the movement of iron ore from the lake boats to the mills located along its route in the Pittsburgh area. The PRR established a large ore dock on Whiskey Island, just west of the Cuyahoga River. Whiskey Island was not a natural island, but the result of the digging of a new and straighter mouth of the Cuyahoga in 1827; Whiskey Island was the land between the natural and man-made mouths of the river. The PRR employed four Hulett cranes to unload the ore boats at the C&P Dock. The Hulett unloaders were at work unloading the *Walter A. Sterling* at Whiskey Island in August 1966. This boat was later purchased by the Ford Motor Company and renamed the *William Clay Ford*.

(Left) A visit to the Pennsylvania's Kinsman Street Yard in Cleveland on June 26, 1965 found a sparkling trio of GE U25Cs, typical of the heavy power assigned to Cleveland. The PRR became a convert to six-axle power in the mid-1960s, with the U25Cs helping to lead the way. The Pennsy purchased 20 out of a total of 113 U25Cs built by General Electric, all contructed in 1965. These three units were part of the first order of ten built in April of that year, so the hard work of moving ore from Cleveland to the mills has not yet dulled their shiny Brunswick green paint.

(Right) Also on hand at Kinsman Street on June 26, 1965 was Bangor & Aroostook GP7 74 in the attractive blue and gray scheme it was delivered in. When ore traffic was at its peak in the summer months, the PRR leased a number of Geeps from the BAR to work the Whiskey Island docks. It was a mutually beneficial relationship, as the BAR traffic was heaviest in the winter months when the lakes were iced over. The arrangement between the two roads was worked out in 1954, allowing the Maine road to purchase enough units to avoid leasing New Haven units in the busy winter season, and enabling the PRR to have sufficient power to work the docks in the summer. This picture was taken over 10 years after the deal was worked out, so it seems to have been a success.

(Above) An eastbound (compass direction southeast) PRR train was crossing Alexander Road in Walton Hills, Ohio on August 29, 1964. An A/B pair of Baldwin Sharks, RF16 9599 leading, assisted a foursome of EMD units out of the Cleveland area. Sharks were common around Cleveland on the PRR as both road power and helpers. The 9599 was one the 30 A/B/A sets of RF16s bought by PRR in 1951/52; it would be retired two years after this shot, in the summer of 1966.

(Below) Chrysler Corporation built a large parts plant at Twinsburg, Ohio in the 1960s. A branchline was built to serve the plant, leaving the PRR's C&P line at Macedonia, Ohio. Baldwin AS616 8974 was in charge of a local on the branch, crossing over Valley View Road heading for Twinsburg in June 1966. The 8974 was used to working solo, as it was one of the AS616s built for hump service. This may be one of its last runs; it was off the roster on July 2, 1966.

(Left) Train #53, the westbound FORT PITT, crossed the skewed bridge over the icy Tuscarawas River at Massillon, Ohio on February 12, 1967. Massillon, eight miles west of Canton, is an industrial city served at this time by the PRR's Pittsburgh/Chicago main line.

(Below) The westbound FORT PITT paused at the Canton, Ohio station on May 19, 1967. Both the faded colors of the E units and the rather forlorn appearance of the station are reminders that travel by rail was in serious decline in the 1960s. The Canton station was at South Market Street.

PC at Collinwood

(Left) Having looked at the operations of its predecessor roads, the New York Central and Pennsylvania, let's take a look at the result of their merger, the ill-starred Penn Central. Actually taken a year into the acquisition of PC by Conrail, a string of PC engines includes a harbinger of the new era in the form of a blue-painted Conrail GE unit in the middle of this remarkable string of first-generation PC units. Cleveland was known as a great location to find F units long after they had become rare or extinct elsewhere. Looking west from the East 152nd Street bridge, the light power move was about to enter the P-1a complex. The coal dock still stands today, but the engine terminal area has been converted to a Flexi-Flo terminal. This shot was taken June 15, 1977.

(Right) Action at QD: an eastbound van train behind a pair of GP30s – the second still in New York Central paint – enters Collinwood Yard on the Lakefront line while two former NYC F7s cool their heels on the Short Line waiting their turn to enter the yard on April 12, 1970.

(Left) The Short Line was the favored routing for heavy drag freights between Berea and Collinwood. A good example is this eastbound unit coal train dropping off the Short Line at QD behind a trio of Alco C636s on June 11, 1972. Each of these units exerted 3,600 horsepower, so this train has plenty of power up front. The 636 didn't find many sales, as few railroads expected Alco to stay in business; the 15 on the Penn Central represented almost half of the total of 34 built.

(Above) A westbound van train was moving out of the yard on July 25, 1971 behind GP38s for power.

5607
5607
5696
5696

Bridging the Cuyahoga

(Left) Bridge 1 is at the man-made mouth of the Cuyahoga River. DB Tower is visible at the far right of this shot as a westbound van train behind GP40 3220 crosses the Cuyahoga on the Lakefront line with downtown Cleveland in the background on August 22, 1976, a few months into the Conrail era.

(Above) On July 22, 1972 an eastbound freight was crossing the Cuyahoga on Bridge 2 on the former Big Four main line. The train will join the Lakefront line at DB Tower for the run through Cleveland to Collinwood Yard. The Cuyahoga takes a roundabout route to the lake in the 80 miles from its source east of Cleveland . It rises in the hills about 35 miles east of the city and flows southwest to Cuyahoga Falls, turning then to a northward direction toward Cleveland, where a series of sharp loops leads to its mouth at Lake Erie. Its curving route through Cleveland requires a large number of bridges, some at river level over just the stream itself, others at higher levels bridging the entire Cuyahoga Valley between the east and west sides of the city.

(Left) The Penn Central's C636s were common sights in Cleveland throughout the Penn Central era. On January 16, 1972 C636 6341 led an ex-NYC U25B over the drawbridge at DB. The track crossing in the right foreground is the Baltimore & Ohio line from West 3rd Street.

6326 6326
GO BROWNS

(Left) Looking west from the Hickory Street overpass we see an eastbound ore train ready to leave the PRR C&P Dock on Whiskey Island bound for Mingo Junction, Ohio on September 12, 1971. It will access the former PRR C&P line through former NYC trackage at DB. A pair of six-axle Alco Centuries was joined by a Southern Pacific SD40 for the run south to the steel mills on the Ohio River.

(Right) Westbound train #63 passed Old Broadway, east of Cleveland Union Terminal, on March 27, 1971. The somber PC black scheme has replaced the gray cigar band paint on the pair of E8s. The tracks passing overhead are the N&W's lead to its East 9th Street Yard.

(Left) Viewed from the West 9th Street overpass, a westbound passed Cleveland Municipal Stadium on May 12, 1973 behind a pair of PC EMDs with GP38-2 8009 leading. The huge stadium by the lake, built in 1931, had a seating capacity of over 77,000, often filled to capacity for Cleveland Browns football games but rarely so for those of the hapless Cleveland Indians in their last years playing at Municipal Stadium. The fortunes of the Indians turned for the better after their move to newly built Jacobs Field, and the original Browns team left Cleveland for Baltimore. The current Browns now use a new stadium in downtown Cleveland; the old Municipal Stadium was demolished in January 1997.

*(Above & Below)*Westbound #63 has finished its work at CUT on March 27, 1971 and is crossing the Cuyahoga Valley Viaduct on the CUT Line. The scene affords a panoramic view of downtown Cleveland. The two scenes show how Cleveland is cut in two by the Cuyahoga Valley, with the downtown section built on the higher ground east of the winding river. The Cuyahoga makes a big loop west of the Terminal, requiring the viaduct that allows the railroad line to parallel the river before finally bridging it. The EL hoppers below alongside the river are on the EL line leading to its ore dock on Whiskey Island.

(Above) Most of the F units that stuck around Cleveland into the 1960s and 1970s were former New York Central F7s. But the PRR F unit fleet had a few survivors that lingered into the Penn Central era as well. One of the former PRR FP7s, the 4332, presented an incongruous look leading a collection of newer PC units through Berea on an eastbound Big Four train on August 3, 1969.

(Below) An eastbound intermodal train swung by BE Tower at Berea on May 9, 1976. In the years since the Penn Central merger, a number of changes had taken place that are shown by this train: trailers on flatcars have replaced the Central's Flexi-vans, and six-axle road switchers like the first two GEs on this train tread rails that saw mostly four-axle diesels in NYC days.

Perry

(Below, Both) Perry, Ohio, on the eastern fringe of greater Cleveland, was named for the region's greatest military hero, Oliver Hazard Perry, who triumphed over the British in the Battle of Lake Erie on September 10, 1813, a victory that helped end the War of 1812 on terms favorable to the United States. On June 20, 1970 eastbound auto rack train ML-12 was speeding down the straight right-of-way along the shore of Lake Erie, with bi-level cars loaded with vans and trucks ahead of tri-levels with new Chevy Novas for east coast buyers. Perry was also the interchange point with the Fairport, Painesville & Eastern.

C430s

(Above) The 10 C430s bought by the New York Central in 1967 were intended to be van-train power, but ended up joining other modern PC Alcos in the Cleveland area after the merger. The 2057 showed off its massive lines leading a GP35 on ex-PRR tracks in Hudson, Ohio in October 1970.

The New York Central's C430 fleet was by far the largest, with only 16 C430s built in total: two to the Reading, one to Green Bay & Western, and the three demonstrators going to the Seaboard Coast Line (later transferred to the Louisville & Nashville).

(Right) Back on ex-New York Central tracks at Perry, C430 2053 had a westbound freight rolling under the signal bridge with a great consist of power to please almost any railfan: not only the rare lead unit, but the only C424 on Penn Central, former PRR unit 2415, a GP9 and an F7. The 2053 was later acquired by the New Jersey shortline Morristown & Erie, renumbered 17 and given a bright-red coat of paint. The photo was taken on April 1, 1973.

Willoughby

(Below) Many F units found their final days on assignment at Cleveland. At Willoughby, roughly 20 miles east of Cleveland, the Willoughby Turn is ready to deliver a unit coal train to the Cleveland Electric Illuminating Eastlake power plant. The 1730 led the train eastbound at Erie Street on February 24, 1974.

Former PRR SD45 6131 lead a westbound around the sweeping super-elevated curve at Erie Street in Willoughby on March 24, 1974, carrying a little snow on its snout from an early spring snowstorm.

Mixing and Matching

(Above) On the third day of Conrail operations, April 3, 1976, the impact of the merger was already apparent as an EL-powered train crossed over the Cuyahoga at DB Tower, heading west on the Lakefront Line.

(Below) Conrail was created on April 1, 1976, merging six bankrupt eastern lines. Cleveland was west of all the affected roads except the Penn Central and Erie Lackawanna, so the primary (but, as we will see, not the only) effect of the government-sponsored move was to bring locomotives from the predecessor roads to the Cleveland area, and to see PC and EL units operating on each other's routes. An example of this was Penn Central units moving over the EL main line at Sharpsville, Pennsylvania on May 1, 1977. The cut at Sharpsville, just over the Ohio border, was created after line relocation around the Shenango River Lake.

(Right) From the standpoint of Cleveland area railfans one of the best results of the Conrail affair was the clustering of big Alco power from the predecessor roads at Cleveland and Mingo Junction, using their low-speed power to move mineral traffic to and from the Cleveland docks. On June 12, 1976 a pair of C628s, ex-PC 6304 and Lehigh Valley 635, was coming off the east leg of the Big Four wye at the east end of DB interlocking.

(Right) A pair of former EL units, U33C 6574 with only CR initials marring its EL paint scheme and an SDP45 repainted into Conrail blue, descended into the Cuyahoga River Valley at Abbey Avenue in Cleveland with an eastbound train of empty ore cars on April 25, 1978.

(Below) The Canadian National detoured trains through the U. S. in the fall of 1976 during tunnel work on the Port Huron, Michigan to Sarnia, Ontario bore. A trio of CN units made an attractive sight as they and their train crossed Bridge 1 at DB, viewed from a yard tower on Whiskey Island. The white buildings of the U. S. Coast Guard station mark the mouth of the Cuyahoga River. The blue waters of Lake Erie stretch out to the horizon on this clear late-fall day, November 14, 1976.

(Right) An eastbound hopper train on the PRR's C&P line passed under the bridge of the abandoned Lake Erie & Pittsburgh line, a former New York Central property, at scenic Brady Lake, Ohio on October 29, 1977. Typical of the heavy mineral trains on this line, the power is a foursome of six-axle Centuries drawn from Conrail predecessor lines, led by repainted C630 6770, a former PRR/PC unit. The yellow paint on the third unit identifies it as one of the 12 C630s inherited from the Reading.

(Left) The Erie Lackawanna also provided Conrail with a fleet of Alco power. The newest of the group were the 12 C425s that joined the road in 1964; along with 15 similar C424s purchased in 1963 they were the only modern Alcos on the EL. Youngstown was a center of Alco activity on the EL, and not much had changed except the letters in the diamond herald on the nose of the 2488, one of the C424s, leading two other Centuries on a short westbound freight bound for Ashtabula on May 22, 1977. The shot was taken at the Hubbard Road crossing in Youngstown.

(Below) Passing the crossing shanty at Hubbard Road in Youngstown on this same May 22, 1977 was this eastbound freight from Ashtabula led by the 8089, a GP38-2 of PC lineage.

(Above) Perhaps the most improbable locomotive to receive Conrail blue paint was F7 1648. It was remarkable that several of the venerable covered wagons survived until 1976, let alone figured in the future plans of the new road. Cleveland was the place to go to find Fs on Conrail, as shown by this train led by the 1648 on May 15, 1977. The train is a westbound transfer from Collinwood to Motor Yard and was shot at Mayfield Road in the Little Italy section of Cleveland. The two close tracks are the N&W's former Nickel Plate main line to Buffalo. The third track is all that remains of the once-electrified CUT line.

(Below) The graceful arches of the NYC bridge over the Grand River at Painesville, Ohio provide a setting for a matched A/B/A set of F7s on June 5, 1976. The New York Central acquired over 300 F units, so perhaps it isn't so surprising that so many lasted into the 1970s. The lead unit, the 1854, was one of the last of the group, joining the roster in 1952. The highway bridge in the foreground carries U. S. Route 20 over the river.

The 1648 led its train past Harvard Tower on the ex-PRR C&P line, crossing the former Wheeling & Lake Erie line of N&W and the Newburgh & South Shore in southeast Cleveland on May 15, 1977. Conrail inherited 161 active F units in 1976, but this unit, later renumbered 1792, was the only one to get the blue paint.

1648
CR
CR

Passenger Operations

(Right) As I mentioned in the introduction, the Nickel Plate was the setting for my first railroad photograph, and it remained a favorite. On July 4, 1961 I got this shot of a pair of PA1s led by the 184 on train #6 at Beidler Road in Willoughby, Ohio. The tight, low angle was an attempt to emulate Howard Fogg's painting from his series of promotion paintings done for the American Locomotive Company in the 1940s and 1950s. The Nickel Plate owned 11 of the Alco units, nicknamed "Blue Birds" for their attractive color scheme.

(Above & Left) At dawn of a September day in 1963 train #6 arrived at Rocky River, Ohio, west of Cleveland, behind GP9 482. By this date the PA1s were gone, traded to Alco for new road switchers. The light was just beginning to illuminate the scene as I turned to shoot the rear end of the train as the passengers boarded the train for Cleveland and points east. The fluted sides of the cars picked up the dim light nicely, and the distinctive gold lettering on the blue stripe above the windows added to the scene.

Nickel Plate Freight Power

(Left) The Nickel Plate added to the Alco scene around Cleveland with a fleet of Alco switchers and road switchers in addition to the PA1s. The 873 led an eastbound through the residential area on the west side of Cleveland at West 110th Street on February 12, 1966. The 873 was a 1,800 horsepower RS36 built in 1962 from a PA1 trade-in.

(Left) NKP 866 led the *Saucer 2* at Conneaut, Ohio on July 19, 1964. The 866 was another of the 11 RS36s purchased after the trade-in of a like number of PA1s.

(Below) The Nickel Plate rostered six-axle power from EMD and Alco for the former Wheeling & Lake Erie coal lines in southern Ohio. The road acquired SD9s and RSD12s in 1957 for trains like this one heading east from Brewster, Ohio on August 2, 1964. Brewster was at the intersection of the old W&LE's two main lines, from Toledo and Cleveland.

Action in Cleveland

(Above) Fairly early in my train-shooting period the Nickel Plate was merged into the Norfolk & Western in 1964. Prior to the NKP acquisition the N&W didn't make it to northern Ohio, with its closest terminus at Columbus. On February 27, 1971 the former NKP engine facility of its main line at East 75th Street in Cleveland hosted two former NKP units, GP9 2466 and RS11 2860. After the merger with the N&W, former Nickel Plate units were given the digit 2 in front of the NKP number, and Wabash units a 3.

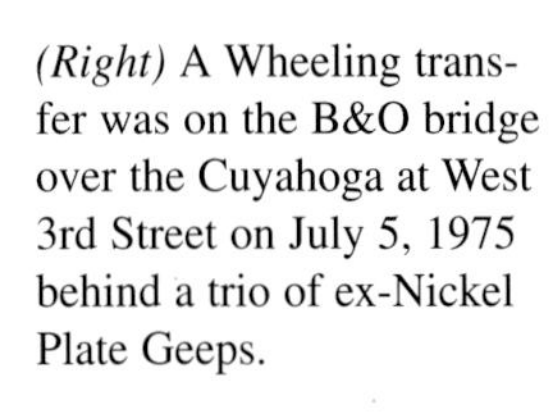

(Right) A Wheeling transfer was on the B&O bridge over the Cuyahoga at West 3rd Street on July 5, 1975 behind a trio of ex-Nickel Plate Geeps.

(Above) A Wheeling transfer from Campbell Road Yard moved east on the EL ore dock line on June 17, 1972. The semaphore signal visible at the left of the tracks is a give-away that this is former Erie Railroad trackage. The train is passing the Sohio refinery en route to the EL East 55th Street yard.

(Below) An eastbound with some mixed freight and intermodal cars passed Mayfield Road in the Little Italy section of Cleveland on June 27, 1974. At this time, one track was still in place on the former CUT line. Little Italy is one of the most vibrant of the many ethnic neighborhoods in Cleveland.

(Below) An eastbound with Cotton Belt and Southern Pacific pool power was heading toward Buffalo on February 4, 1973 at old Broadway Avenue. The 52-story Terminal Tower is directly above the train as it passes the catenary towers formerly used by Cleveland Union Terminal motors.

(Below) After the LV was folded into Conrail in the spring of 1976, the expanded D&H took over operation of the run-through piggyback trains. The eastbound *Apollo-2* was passing through East 34th Street on July 18, 1976 behind two D&H EMDs and an N&W GP35. The lead unit, the 7408, is a former Reading GP39-2 and the 7323 a former Lehigh Valley GP38-2. The arrival of the D&H power added significantly to the color of railroading in Cleveland. The Sohio refinery is in the background, a reminder of how important oil refining was to the growth of Cleveland.

(Below) Euclid is a suburb east of Cleveland, roughly 12 miles from downtown. The former NKP line to Buffalo heads in a northeasterly direction through Euclid and comes again close to the NYC main line after taking a more southerly route through Cleveland. At Euclid an unusual unit, re-engined Baldwin road switcher 7902, was switching the yard on March 24, 1974. The former NKP 322 was one of four Baldwin AS16 units owned by the NKP, all of which were re-engined in 1959. The 322 and 323 got EMD prime movers and the 320 and 321 Alco 251's.

(Above) GP35 1327 appears to have recently received a new coat of black paint that really stands out in the snow at Chardon Road in Euclid, leading a westbound on February 5, 1983. Alco T6 29 was the switcher assigned to Euclid this wintry day.

Chagrin Falls Branch

(Above) The former Wheeling & Lake Erie branch to Chagrin Falls usually rated two or three Alco switchers, drawn from the large stable of Schenectady-built S1-4s owned by the Nickel Plate and inherited by the N&W. A south-bound trio has received clearance to cross the EL's Cleveland-Youngstown line at Solon, Ohio on May 19, 1972. Lead unit 2060 is an S4, formerly Nickel Plate 60, built in 1951. The branch was eight miles in length, from Falls Junction in Glenwillow to the terminus at Chagrin Falls; Solon was three miles from Falls Junction.

(Below) The end of the line at Chagrin Falls. The N&W freight station at Chagrin Falls still showed the NKP's gray paint and signage on May 29, 1967. Bill Surdyk ran the last train to Chagrin Falls in the spring of 1986. Today the branch terminates at Solon, where it services an industrial park.

The N&W at Willoughby

(Right) Willoughby, 20 miles east of Cleveland, was served by both the NYC/PC and NKP/N&W. On June 25, 1966 a set of ex-Wabash units, U25B 3518 and an F7A, crossed the Chagrin River at Willoughby with a westbound freight. The hilly terrain along the Lake Erie shoreline in the Cleveland area made it necessary for the NKP to construct a large number of impressive bridges to span the many rivers flowing into the lake.

(Below) At Erie Street in Willoughby Tuscan Red SD40-2 6175, the only such unit to receive this paint scheme, was on the point running long-end forward on an eastbound train on January 23, 1982. The old Willoughby Coal & Supply building still stands today, a modeler's dream for a distinctive trackside structure.

Painesville

(Above) Painesville is an elegant old community 30 miles east of Cleveland, situated on the plateau above Lake Erie near the mouth of the Grand River. Westbound train TC-1 was crossing Liberty Street in Painesville on May 10, 1975.

(Above) Westbound NE-1 passed PE Tower at Painesville on May 8, 1976 behind a pair of brand-new Delaware & Hudson GP39-2s, so new that the logos have not yet been applied. It's just over a month since the D&H assumed the role formerly played by the Lehigh Valley on run-through freights like NE-1.

(Right) Westbound freight CN-90 passed Woodworth Farm Supply in Painesville on August 3, 1985.

(Right) The Nickel Plate employed mostly four-axle freight power in the years before the N&W merger, but the N&W era saw more and more six-axle power. Two of the biggest of the N&W's diesel fleet, SD45s 1779 and an unidentified mate, passed the old Nickel Plate station at Painesville heading toward Buffalo on February 15, 1981.

(Right) PE Tower controlled the crossing of the B&O Fairport Branch and the Nickel Plate main line. This was a steam hot spot into the late 1950s, with Nickel Plate Berkshires and B&O EM1s working well past the time when other roads had finished dieselization. I was at PE Tower to shoot this westbound with a block of auto parts boxcars up front from a window in the tower on July 29, 1972.

Grand River Bridge

(Above) The photographic highlight of Painesville is the soaring trestle over the Grand River. A set of first-generation EMDs was crossing the steel trestle with an eastbound on May 8, 1976.

(Below) The N&W/Lehigh Valley partnership was on display at the Grand River Bridge on September 24, 1972 as a high-nosed N&W GP35 led two "Yellowjacket" LV C420s on eastbound NWL-2. The Lehigh Valley Alcos were in pool service between Bellevue, Ohio and Buffalo.

Cleveland Revisited

(Left) By 1985, things were continuing to change on the former Nickel Plate in Cleveland. Norfolk & Western was giving way to Norfolk Southern after the merger between N&W and Southern Railway. The third unit of this set of EMDs heading east at Abbey Avenue in Cleveland bears the new road's lettering and "Thoroughbred" logo while the first two units sport different approaches to N&W black and white.

(Above) The Norfolk & Western got into the Bicentennial spirit quite early, painting SD45 1776 into this attractive red, white and blue color scheme. It led westbound freight TC-1 past the old West 110th Street Yard on August 24, 1974.

(Below) Rocky River is a suburb of Cleveland just shy of nine miles west of Cleveland. As its name indicates, the community is located where the Rocky River empties into Lake Erie. Another of the NKP steel bridges spans the muddy Rocky River and provides the setting for this shot of Union Pacific SD40s 3050 and 3190 in pool power service leading a westbound on February 4, 1973.

(Right) Barreling past the station at Rocky River on March 26, 1973 was this westbound freight led by Alco C628s 1119 and 1125. The N&W rostered 30 of the high-nosed C628s, 1100-1129. Soon after this shot was taken, the fleet was leased and then sold to the Chicago & North Western, spending most of their time on ore trains in the Upper Peninsula of Michigan. The 1119 was renumbered 6720 by the North Western, and served its new owner until being retired and then scrapped in 1990.

First Generation Diesels

(Above) The Nickel Plate put a group of 23 RS3s into service in 1954. They remained well into the N&W era and in later years were used in yard service. Two of the group, the 2556 and 2555, worked at Center Street at the west end of the yard at Bellevue, Ohio on April 23, 1967.

(Below) The N&W merged with the Virginian in 1959 and acquired in the process the VGN's sizeable group of Fairbanks-Morse road switchers. A pair of the Virginian H16-44s led a train on the former Wheeling & Lake Erie over the PRR at Wandle Tower in Canton, Ohio in November 1966.

ERIE LACKAWANNA

East 55th Street Engine Terminal

(Above) The Erie Lackawanna did not have the same presence in Cleveland as the New York Central and Nickel Plate, but it did have its headquarters there, in the Midland Building in downtown Cleveland, a legacy of the Erie Railroad's ownership by the Van Sweringen brothers. E8 825 rode the turntable at the East 55th Street engine terminal on March 22, 1976. The unit was used as power on the remaining EL passenger service out of Cleveland, trains 28/29 between Cleveland and Youngstown.

(Right) Century 425 2456, C424 2401, and a third Century pause on the turntable at East 55th Street on the night of May 23, 1970. The EL invested quite heavily in Alco products in its early years, buying 15 C424s in 1963 and 12 C425s in the following year.

(Right) A real potpourri of power was resting at East 55th Street on May 3, 1969, with former Lackawanna Train Master 1860 in the black and yellow early EL scheme sharing the space with a variety of Alco units.

(Left) The EL operated its own ore dock at a cramped location along the Cuyahoga not far inland from the PRR's C&P Dock. It utilized three Huletts to unload the ore from the boats. To move the heavy ore trains out of Cleveland the EL used its heaviest power, in this case three ex-Lackawanna Train Masters. The EL inherited 12 Train Masters from the Lackawanna, and they were commonly found in Cleveland in the 1960s.

 Train Masters

(Left) The Train Masters were gradually repainted from the black and yellow into the yellow/maroon/gray EL scheme that was reminiscent of the colors they wore on the DL&W. The 1854 led two other units south passing under the Detroit-Superior High Bridge on June 9, 1968, leaving a trail of the bluish-gray smoke that was characteristic of Fairbanks-Morse units.

(Below) The EL ore dock in Cleveland was cramped, leaving little room for storage of ore or excess cars. To keep the dock functional, the EL often moved loaded cuts of hoppers 11 miles down the line to North Randall, where they would be combined to form trains for Youngstown. A trio of Train Masters is heading south at East 55th Street with loads; the date is July 1965.

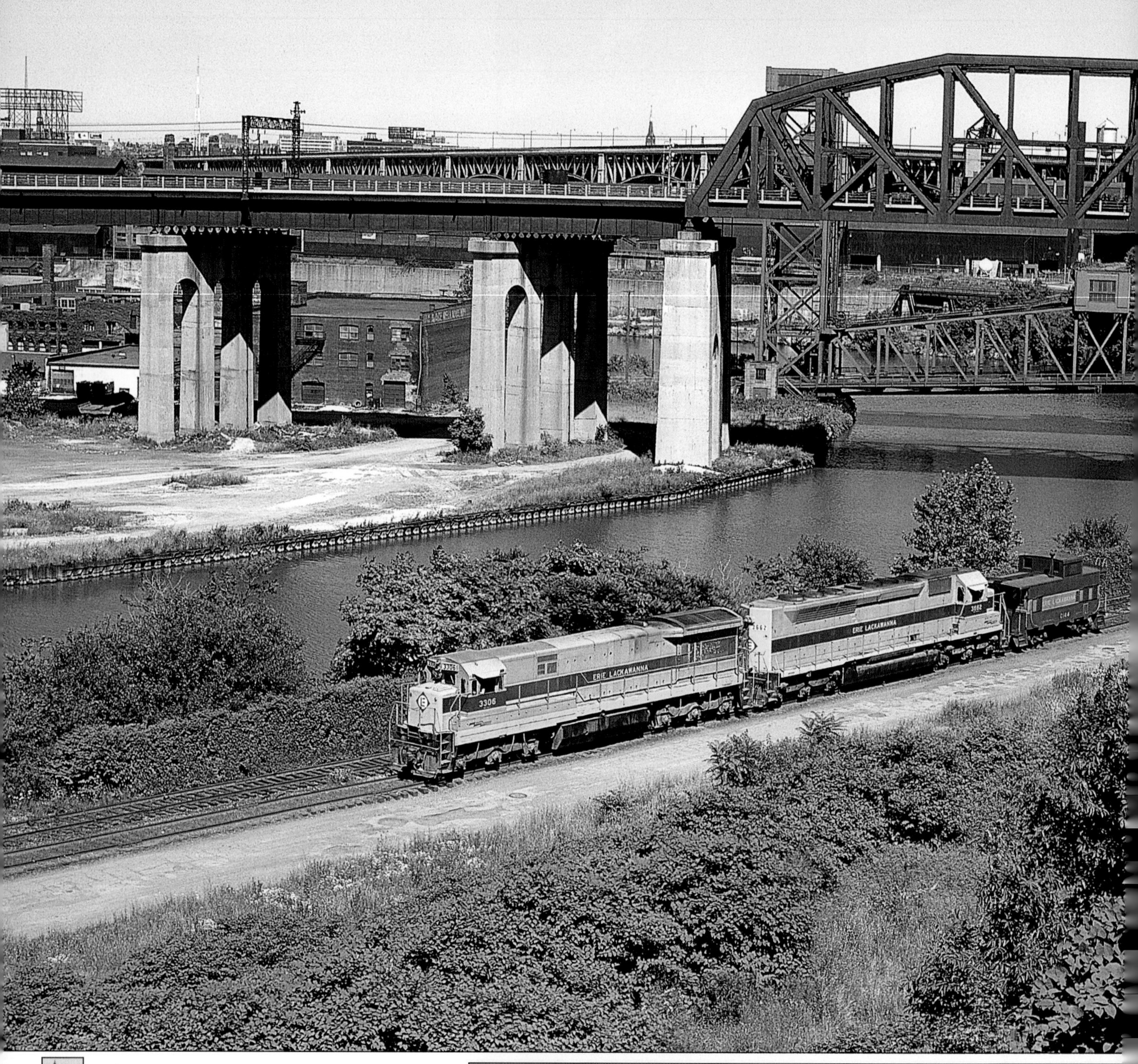

In the Second Generation

(Above) The Train Masters were replaced by second-generation units, usually six-axle types like the U33C and SDP45 seen on July 20, 1974 on a caboose hop from East 55th Street to the ore dock to pick up a train. This scene was recorded from the bluffs on West 25th Street near Bridge Avenue along one of the big twists in the Cuyahoga.

(Right) The units seen running light along the Cuyahoga, SDP45 3662 and U33C 3306, picked up their train at the ore dock and were departing for Youngstown.

Train #28

(Below) Trains #28 and #29 were essentially commuter trains serving the corridor between Cleveland and Youngstown. Train #28 was scheduled out of Cleveland Union Terminal at 5:20 PM daily except Saturday, taking one hour and 50 minutes to cover the 13 stops and 66.2 miles to Youngstown. On March 22, 1976 #28 backed down to Cleveland Union Terminal from the East 55th Street Yard at MR Junction. In the right background is the N&W's former Nickel Plate East 55th Street Yard.

(Right) The Cleveland/Youngstown trains of the EL were the last passenger trains operated out of CUT. Weeds were overtaking most of the area in the 1970s as #28 headed out of the terminal under the still-imposing Terminal Tower. The shot was taken at East 9th Street on August 31, 1972.

(Above & Below) EL #28 moved south at old Broadway Avenue in May 1971 under the old catenary towers. This panorama shows the N&W's East 9th Street Yard on the upper level and the N&W mainline to Buffalo to the left of the EL train. In the going away shot, all kinds of activity is going on as #28 accelerates toward Youngstown. An Alco S4 switcher is working the 9th Street Yard on the upper level while three RS3s are switching on the main line. It's May 1971 but all the power dates well back to the early diesel days.

(Left) The EL acquired 15 U33Cs and 13 U36Cs between 1968 and 1972. The GE units were well-suited to the heavy ore service out of Cleveland, and showed up frequently. The last of the U33Cs, the 3315, had a train of empty hoppers returning to the docks at Solon, Ohio, 15.5 miles south of Cleveland, on May 22, 1971.

(Above) At Mantua, 29.7 miles south of CUT, train #28 skirted a man-made lake on May 12, 1972.

On the Main Line

(Above) The former Erie Railroad main line of the EL passed south of the Cleveland metropolitan region but was close enough for many fruitful visits. One of the closest spots was Kent, 594.2 miles west of the eastern terminus of the EL at Hoboken, New Jersey and about 40 miles south of Cleveland. U36C 3316, the first of the 13 of its type delivered in 1972, still looked new as it led an eastbound through the yard at Kent on January 21, 1973.

(Above) On February 7, 1976 two EL Bicentennial units, SDP45 3638 and SD45, led eastbound NY-100 over the PRR's C&P Branch at Brady Lake, Ohio. Being careful not to leave footprints in the snow, it was a cold wait of about an hour to get this shot.

Akron

(Above) Akron, 10 miles west of Kent, is the closest large city to Cleveland and was an important stop for Erie Lackawanna passenger trains. A pair of E8s led westbound Mail #3 out of Akron on May 14, 1966. The fateful decision of the U. S. Postal Service to switch from trains to trucks for inter-city mail movements in 1967 led to the demise of trains like this and passenger trains like THE LAKE CITIES that gathered more revenue from mail contracts than paying passengers.

(Left) Shortly after Mail #3 headed west out of the Akron station, eastbound train #6, THE LAKE CITIES, arrived on its run from Chicago's Dearborn Station to Hoboken. After the flagship EL train, PHOEBE SNOW, was dropped late in 1966, trains 5/6 were the last remaining Hoboken/Chicago trains. The train was not the fastest way to get from Chicago to the New York area, taking 24 hours to make the 977-mile run, but for residents of the many communities along the EL line it was an overnight train offering sleeping car service from Youngstown to Hoboken and a diner from Chicago to Hoboken. A pair of E8s had the assignment on May 14, 1966. If it was on time, it was ten minutes after 7 PM.

Wadsworth

(Above) At Wadsworth, the westbound LAKE CITIES, train #5, received a clear signal from the semaphore as it headed for Chicago on December 17, 1966. With Christmas only a week away, the holiday may have increased the size of the train, which is running a healthy seven cars.

(Below) The roof of the Wadsworth station is just visible above the cars as THE LAKE CITIES passed, but Wadsworth was not a scheduled stop for the train. The train was scheduled through Akron at 10:05 AM and due in Chicago at 4:30 PM.

Sterling

(Above) Sterling, Ohio was a busy spot, with the EL crossing the Baltimore & Ohio main line at grade on a sharp angle. The crossing was controlled by RU Tower, staffed by the EL. A pair of SDP45s headed east over the B&O on April 15, 1973. The EL operated 34 of these units, with the longer size permitting a larger fuel tank than regular SD45s.

(Below) Signal failure at Sterling on April 15, 1973 caused an interesting delay. Delaware & Hudson C628 612 with three EL units had a light power move in tow. A westbound mixed freight pulled alongside, powered by GP35s. The D&H unit was one of several seen working on the EL in the spring and summer of 1973.

Lima

(Above) Lima is 155 miles west of Akron in northwestern Ohio. On November 25, 1967 I made a circle trip by train. Starting in Crestline, Ohio I took the New York Central MIAMI VALLEY BEELINER with a Budd RDC car to Galion, where I caught westbound EL #5 to take me to Lima. At Lima, I got a Pennsylvania Railroad train to get me back to Crestline. EL #5 is pictured here at Lima in the early afternoon with an Illinois Central baggage car in the consist. The distant headlight indicated another westbound EL movement was waiting for #5 to head out of town, as we see in the next shot.

This was definitely THE shot of the day. Waiting for #5 to clear the station at Lima, seven of EL's 14 PAs and two FBs were stopped east of the B&O crossing on November 25, 1967.

Youngstown

(Above) Let's head back east on the EL main to Youngstown, a busy spot on the EL and the center of the steel industry in the Mahoning Valley. In its heyday as a steel-making center, the 25-mile stretch of the valley near the Ohio/Pennsylvania boundary was called "America's Ruhr" for its resemblance to the great industrial region in Germany. The Big Four eastern railroads – Pennsylvania, New York Central, B&O, and Erie – all served Youngstown, with the Erie Lackawanna having a good share of the local business. An eastbound local freight at Hazel Street in Youngstown had Baldwin S12 627 and Lima-Hamilton 659 on the day after Christmas, December 26, 1965. The 659 was one of ten 1,000 horsepower Lima switchers bought by the Erie in 1949; the Erie also had six 1,200 Lima switchers, one of the few roads to buy diesels from the Ohio builder.

(Above) A westbound crossed the New York Central's Ashtabula line at Valley Street interlocking in Youngstown on June 24, 1967 with GP7 1220 leading an RS3.

EL 2411, a C424, led this westbound at Westlake Crossing in Youngstown on February 18, 1968, having picked up some snow on its pilot this winter day.

66-2M

(Above) An eastbound freight at Westlake Crossing had an A/B/A set of weary-looking F units on June 20, 1971.

(Right) At DeForest Junction at Niles, Ohio, the EL crossed the Fairport Harbor line of the B&O. This location was just over 8 miles west of Youngstown. DeForest Junction was so named because two B&O lines, the Lake Subdivision between Youngstown and Fairport Harbor and the Newton Falls Subdivision connected there. RT Tower just west of the B&O junction controlled the diamond of the Lake Sub and the Erie Lackawanna. On May 4, 1968 an F3 led a Century and a U25B past the tower at the crossing; the tower still wears the identifying letter "P" used during the Erie Railroad era.

(Above) Westbound mail train #3 crossed Valley Street in Youngstown on June 14, 1967.

(Below) The Lake Cities was westbound at Valley Street in June 1969. The three E8s and long train belie the fact that time is running out for intercity trains on the EL. The last run of trains 5/6 came about six months later on January 6, 1970. The EL inherited E8s from both the Erie and the Lackawanna; the lead unit 821 was a former Erie unit.

(Left) The Erie, P&LE and B&O cooperated on passenger trains between Cleveland, Pittsburgh, and Washington. In July 1960 the morning eastbound train on this run, THE STEEL KING, arrived at the Youngstown station behind an Erie RS3 and three gray and green cars. It is still a few months to go before the merger with the Lackawanna is consummated on October 17, 1960.

(Above) Even though the EL's passenger patronage was dwindling in the 1960s, it still enjoyed a flourishing package and express business. Witness the large collection of boxes entrusted to the baggage handlers by Train #7 at Youngstown on August 31, 1962.

(Right) Seen from the cab of the RS3 leading train #628, the Erie/EL line ran down gauntlet tracks on U. S. Route 422 in Warren, Ohio. The sign in the background announces the price of gas as 29.9 cents, showing how difficult it was for the railroad to compete with the automobile. Warren is 14 miles north of Youngstown.

(Below) Train #28 with matched EL equipment made a nice sight in the evening light at Girard, Ohio on May 21, 1973. The train was reputedly losing around $200,000 a year, but pressure from riders (many of them pass holders) kept the Public Utility Commission of Ohio (PUCO) from approving its discontinuance.

Harris
Flower Shop
4014
CR
RADIO EQUIPPED

(Left) The end of passenger service on the EL (by then Conrail) line between Cleveland and Youngstown came on January 14, 1977. E8 4014 paused in the winter darkness at Youngstown with the last #28. The Forest City Division of the Railroad Enthusiasts arranged a night photo session for the last run as an era ended in northeast Ohio railroading.

Valley Line

(Above) The Baltimore & Ohio reached Cleveland on two lines, the CT&V Subdivision from Akron and the Cleveland Subdivision from Lester. The two lines merged at C&TV Junction on the south side of Cleveland, where RD Tower controlled the interlocking and also the crossing of the N&W's former W&LE Cleveland Belt Line Branch. The CT&V Sub derived its name from the predecessor line that built up the Cuyahoga Valley in the late 19th century, the Cleveland Terminal & Valley, which was absorbed by the B&O in 1915. The CT&V Sub followed the largely undeveloped and scenic Cuyahoga River Valley through an area now designated a national park. On March 17, 1974 an eastbound freight was running down the west bank of the river at Brecksville and passing under the Route 82 bridge with a pair of EMD road switchers for power.

(Right) Chessie System ran a passenger special from Cleveland to Washington, D. C. for President Richard M. Nixon's second inauguration in January 1973. The special was eastbound on the Valley line along Riverview Road in Ira, Ohio on January 21, 1973.

(Below) Although its tracks did not reach Cleveland, the headquarters of the Chesapeake & Ohio were located in the Terminal Tower. When the Chessie System image and logo were unveiled, a press conference was held at the B&O yard at West 3rd Street, not far from the Terminal Tower. GP40-2 1977 displayed the new image on August 31, 1972. Large orders for GP40s and GP40-2s in the late 1960s and 1970s made this type the standard locomotive for the Chessie roads.

(Left) The B&O had a regional office at Canal Road and Carter Road in The Flats. The first floor of the distinctive Victorian-era building had served as the B&O's Cleveland passenger depot until 1934, when the road began using CUT. The building still stands as this is written; there are plans to restore it and use it as a cultural center.

Painesville

(Above) The Lake Subdivision (also called the Lake Branch) extended north from Ohio Junction in Youngstown to Fairport, on the shore of Lake Erie 59 miles north of Youngstown. The line was largely a conduit for mineral traffic but also carried mixed freight for interchange with the other roads at Painesville and Fairport. It crossed the N&W's ex-Nickel Plate main line at PE Tower in Painesville. The brick tower witnessed the crossing of S4 9110 with a local freight on March 16, 1967.

(Right) Trains heading compass south on the Lake Sub were eastbounds. This eastbound with three Geeps has just crossed the N&W at PE Tower and is in the shadows of the cut under the Route 84 bridge in Painesville on November 6, 1972. The Lake Sub was originally a narrow gauge line, the Painesville & Youngstown, and was not built to very high standards. This train is digging in for the 11-mile grade to the town of Chardon that averaged 1.6%, one of several grades on the roller-coaster profile of the subdivision.

(Below) On March 15, 1975 snow dusted the ground as Painesville 97 entered Painesville on the long grade from Chardon. The train was the westbound part of a pair of trains that operated over the branch to and from New Castle, Pennsylvania. It is about to cross the N&W at PE Tower.

(Below) The CL&W Subdivision carried the name of its predecessor railroad, the Cleveland, Lorain & Wheeling, absorbed into the B&O in 1909. It provided access to the large lake port of Lorain from the Akron-Chicago Division main line at Sterling, 39 miles to the south. At Lester, the CL&W met the Cleveland Subdivision, which extended a little over 28 miles to its junction with the Valley Sub at RD Tower. Western Maryland SD40 7473 in the WM's attractive black and gold colors was heading west on the CL&W toward Lorain at Lester on June 6, 1976, after some significant ballast work on the line. The Lester depot is just visible behind the train.

(Right) Both the CL&W and Cleveland subdivisions were important branches, and the depot at Lester was close to their junction. The tracks to the right are the Cleveland Sub and the tracks to the left are the CL&W, curving toward Lorain. A third branch to Medina joined the CL&W at Lester. The shot is looking north and was taken on December 17, 1966.

(Below) At Grafton the CL&W line to Lorain crossed the Big Four line of the New York Central between Cleveland and Columbus. Grafton Tower controlled the crossing. On April 27, 1974 gold-painted GP40-2 GM50 on its way to Lorain passed the tower, a typical Big Four structure mounted on steel supports.

Sterling

(Above) We've already seen the EL in action at Sterling. Let's now turn our attention to the B&O at this busy crossing. This eastbound freight was crossing the EL with RU Tower visible in the background.

(Left & Below) Train #7, THE DIPLOMAT, approached the EL crossing on its westbound run from Washington Union Station to Chicago's Grand Central Station on December 17, 1966. Above the train are visible the signals of each road, color position lights on the B&O and a semaphore blade on the EL. Train #7 was due through Sterling – not a scheduled stop – around 11 AM.

(Above) A westbound was led by GP30 6963 at Arlington Street in Akron on March 10, 1974. The location was called Akron Junction; here the PRR and B&O converged and used a shared double tracks to Warwick, 16 miles to the west. The PRR line to Hudson, Ohio continued east of Akron Junction; it is the track diverging to the left under the third unit of the B&O train.

(Right) Late on an evening in October 1966 I shot train #9, THE CHICAGO EXPRESS, as it paused for the station stop at Akron Union Station, used by the B&O and PRR.

Kent

One of the photogenic locations on the B&O in eastern Ohio was in Kent, where the B&O passed alongside the Cuyahoga River. It was especially beautiful in winter with snow on the ground and ice on the river. GP40 4056 was heading west through downtown Kent; the EL main line is to the right.

Ravenna

(Left) An eastbound freight was passing RN Tower in Ravenna in June 1970. Ravenna was the junction with the PRR's C&P Branch, visible in the background crossing over the B&O. The track curving away to the right is the connection with the C&P that was used by the Pennsylvania to access the B&O between Ravenna and Niles Junction, a way for the PRR to have a more direct route between Cleveland and Youngstown. The C&P itself continued south to a connection with the PRR main line at Alliance. The Ravenna operator is down on the tower stairs for the roll-by. Ravenna is 34 miles west of Youngstown and 19 miles east of Akron.

(Below) An eastbound freight at Chestnut Street in Ravenna rolled under the overpass of the original C&P line through Ravenna behind a set of first-generation EMDs on February 7, 1976. The Chessie System had by this time semi-merged its three constituent roads, the B&O, C&O, and Western Maryland, leading to unusual sights like this set of two WM F7s and a C&O GP9 on B&O rails.

 Youngstown

(Above) Seen from the Market Street Bridge, a pair of Alco cab units led a fascinating collection of boxcars and refrigerator cars west along the Mahoning River in July 1960. The tracks on the upper level belong to the P&LE and NYC's Lake Erie & Eastern line.

(Right) Looking east from Center Street in Youngstown, we see Alco switchers working at Haselton Junction on July 4, 1972. The steel industry in Youngstown was still humming at this time, and holiday or not the railroads and mills are hard at work. The Haselton plant of Republic Steel is in the background, along with a westbound PC train.

(Below) Perhaps the best-known rail location in Youngstown was Center Street Junction. The B&O crossed lines of the NYC, PRR, and EL near the Republic Steel mill. This eastbound was crossing the former PRR tracks as a Conrail train with PC power waited its turn on September 19, 1976.

(Above) Campbell, Ohio, east of Youngstown, was the location of the Youngstown Sheet & Tube steel mill. The mill is in the background of this shot of an eastbound trailer train passing through Campbell behind a pair of new SD40s on May 30, 1967.

(Right) The P&LE's Gateway Yard and main line at Struthers, Ohio, on the eastern outskirts of Youngstown are to the left of an eastbound B&O hopper train on May 30, 1967. The Alco cab units were running out some of their final miles and have lost their original attractive blue and gray scheme in exchange for the simple solid blue with yellow lettering of the 1960s.

4135
B & O
B & O

Youngstown Passenger Station

(Above, Right, & Below) The B&O's passenger station in Youngstown was on the west side of the Mahoning River. Downtown Youngstown was to the east, on the opposite side of the river. On July 3, 1965 westbound train #7 arrived at the Youngstown station on its Washington-Chicago run. After the passengers boarded the train, a classic heavyweight diner brought up the rear as the train resumed its 16-hour run from the nation's capital to Chicago.

(Left) A view of the B&O station at Youngstown in September 1968 shows its elegant lines and stone construction. The station now houses a restaurant as well as serving Amtrak today.

(Left) After its Youngstown station stop on May 30, 1967, train #8 proceeded east. The overhead shot from the Market Street Bridge in Youngstown captures a lot of the look of Youngstown: rail lines, steel mills, and the Mahoning River just visible on the right of the train.

(Right) Train #8, The Shenandoah, arrived at Youngstown on its way east to Washington on May 30, 1967. The low morning light made the solid dark blue units glow a bit. By 1968, train #8's schedule had been cut back to a Pittsburgh to Washington run, with train #10, The Gateway, covering the Chicago to Pittsburgh run. The B&O's premier train, The Capitol Limited, passed through Ohio well after dark in both directions.

(Above) Pittsburgh & Conneaut Docks operated the harbor complex on Lake Erie at Conneaut, Ohio. Conneaut is just west of the Ohio/Pennsylvania state line and was an important port for iron ore destined for the mills of the Pittsburgh region since the 1890s. Over the years, the Conneaut facilities were modernized so that each of the three major commodities used by the steel industry – limestone, coal, and iron ore – had its own dedicated dock, permitting storage as well as loading and unloading at the harbor. An unusual feature of the Conneaut operation was the use of F units by the P&C Dock Company to switch the port. Wearing a dirty coat of yellow and black paint, the P&C's 1 and 2, formerly Bessemer & Lake Erie 715 A/B, were at the four-track swing bridge over Conneaut Creek on May 16, 1971.

(Left) Baldwin road switcher 403 was switching the south end of Conneaut Yard at YA Tower on August 15, 1964. The 403 was a DRS-6-6-15 purchased in 1950 and used primarily for heavy switching duties on the B&LE.

(Above) The Bessemer & Lake Erie was one of the family of railroads owned by U. S. Steel. The USS roads frequently swapped power from one to another. A case in point was the transfer of six Alco RSD15 road switchers from the Duluth, Missabe & Iron Range to the B&LE in 1964. Two of the 2,400 horsepower units led a pair of EMD units under the New York Central main line and into Conneaut Yard on August 15, 1964 with empty ore cars for reloading at Dock Four, the ore dock at Conneaut.

(Above) Albion, Pennsylvania was the junction of the B&LE's lines to Erie, Pennsylvania and Conneaut. From Albion south, trains from both destinations used the B&LE main line to Greenville and North Bessemer, Pennsylvania. Four of the six RSD15s were on the point of this southbound train preparing to leave Albion Yard on June 14, 1964. Albion Yard collected the ore traffic from Conneaut and marshaled coal movements northbound for the port. As the powerful RSD15s settled into their role on the B&LE they were more commonly found on the Albion/Conneaut trains than on main line moves like this. The big Alcos were sent in 1972/73 to another iron ore road, the Cartier Railway in northern Quebec.

(Left) RX Tower in Albion controlled the movements at the end of the B&LE's 135 miles of main line Centralized Traffic Control between this point and XB Tower at North Bessemer. SD18 857 was entering CTC territory as it headed south on May 16, 1971. The train is about to cross Pennsylvania Route 18 on its way to North Bessemer and a connection with another USS road, the Union.

(Below) Osgood, Pennsylvania was a fascinating location. Four rail lines passed through the little community: the New York Central's line between Ashtabula, Ohio and Franklin, Pennsylvania, the Erie/EL main line, and two B&LE lines. The B&LE's Old Line followed the path of the Shenango River, while a bypass line, the 8.8 mile High Line or K-O Line provided a shorter and easier route around Greenville, Pa. On August 6, 1967 nearly new SD38 861 led three older SDs over the Osgood Viaduct, the longest on the railroad. The 861was one of three SD38s acquired in 1967 by the B&LE.

(Below) Moving back to the state of Ohio, let's take a look at the Akron, Canton & Youngstown Railroad. The AC&Y stretched 169.3 miles across northern Ohio, from Mogadore on the east to Delphos on the west. The original line extended a little over 7 miles from Akron to Mogadore, where it connected with the Wheeling & Lake Erie. In 1920 the AC&Y gained control of the Northern Ohio Railroad and its line from Delphos to Akron. This change made the road's name a misnomer, as it turned its sights west instead of east; it never attempted to reach either Canton or Youngstown.

The AC&Y was a hard railroad to categorize, serving as both a bridge route for east/west traffic and as a switching road for the highly industrialized region around the three cities in eastern Ohio that lent their names to its company title. Its headquarters was Akron, where Brittain Yard on the east side of the city was its operating center. It was noted for its roster of Fairbanks-Morse road switchers such as H16-44 203 in brilliant yellow paint and silver trucks, at Brittain Yard on June 24, 1965.

(Below) H16-44 204 rode the turntable at Brittain Yard on May 19, 1967. The 204 was a so-called "Phase II" H16-44. Built in 1954, it had the the square cab windows that differentiated it from the Loewy-designed early units like the 203. Putting the road name on the locomotive frame sill was an unusual touch employed by the AC&Y.

(Below) The 202, another of the early H16-44s, switched the west end of Brittain Yard at Akron on June 24, 1965. Besides its eight H16s, the AC&Y rostered nine H20-44s (including three transferred from another N&W property, the Pittsburgh & West Virginia) and one H15-44. Besides the FMs, the AC&Y had one Alco RS1 and seven Alco S2 switchers.

(Above) Extra 208 West crossed Route 18, the Memorial Parkway, in Akron on April 27, 1968. The second unit is one of the former Pittsburgh & West Virginia H20-44s that had been repainted into N&W blue after the P&WV was merged into the N&W in 1964. The AC&Y was more fortunate than the P&WV in its ability to keep its identity in place and not be swallowed up into the expanding N&W until January 1982, when the AC&Y became another fallen flag road.

(Below) Extra 208 West passed the station at Medina, Ohio, 21.5 miles west of Akron, on April 27, 1968. Medina was also served by a B&O branch from the CL&W at Lester, and interchanged with the AC&Y there. The 208 was a late H16-44 built in 1957, and has the thicker frame sills similar to the Train Master design.

A&BB AKRON & BARBERTON BELT

(Right) The Akron & Barberton Belt Railroad was the brainchild of an Akron industrialist, O. C. Barber, who established industries in the new town of Barberton southwest of Akron and needed a railroad to connect with the trunk lines serving the area. In 1902, the Akron & Barberton Belt was formed and sold shortly afterward for $1 million dollars to a consortium of the Pennsylvania, Baltimore & Ohio, Northern Ohio (later to be acquired by the Akron, Canton & Youngstown), and the Erie. The A&BB had two major lines, one heading north from Barberton to Fairlawn and the other from Barberton to Akron. The road bought four Baldwin diesels new between 1942 and 1952, and also picked up an RS3 second-hand from Penn Central. Baldwin S12 28 was switching at Barberton on August 5, 1967. The 28 was the newest of the four Baldwins. The bold yellow lettering left no question of who the engine worked for; note the unusual use of periods after the letters.

FP&E FAIRPORT, PAINESVILLE & EASTERN

(Left) We've already looked at the NKP/N&W, NYC and B&O around Painesville and Fairport. Let's look at the area's switching and terminal road, the Fairport, Painesville & Eastern. The FP&E had its general headquarters in Painesville. It operated seven Alco switchers, which it began acquiring in 1945; all were 1,000 horsepower units. Two of the units, the 106 and 107, were former Nickel Plate units. S2 101 was at Fairport Harbor on May 5, 1968 sporting the road's logo on the cab, the initials of the road inside a map of Ohio. The 101 was the first of the road's Alco switchers, built in 1945.

(Above) A view of the FP&E yard and office at Fairport Harbor was taken on June 7, 1970. Fairport Harbor was primarily a coal-handling lake port. Its ore business was hindered by out-of-date unloading facilities that could not compete with the more modern facilities at other Lake Erie ports; it was closed as an ore port after World War II. The FP&E had a good deal of business locally, and was not dependent on the fortunes of the lake port.

(Above) A westbound was running alongside Route 535 at Fairport Harbor on January 25, 1967. The first unit is the FP&E's only S4, the 105. The train has a number of tank cars, as one of the major local sources of traffic was the chemicals industry. The green and yellow scheme of the FP&E in the 1960s was one of the most attractive around, especially when the units were as clean as these two.

(Right) In the 1970s the FP&E switched to a darker yellow and black scheme, retaining its map of Ohio herald on the cab sides and adding one on the front of the engine. A pair of S2s, the 104 and 107, switched the west end of the yard at Fairport Harbor on June 7, 1970. The second unit was originally NKP 45, then N&W 2045, before ending up on the FP&E.

(Left) The east end of the FP&E was at Perry, Ohio, where the road had interchanges with the PC (former NYC) and N&W (former NKP). On July 12, 1975 the 103 and another S2 were at the N&W making a set-out. In 1984 the N&W purchased the FP&E and ended its independent existence.

(Right) Compared to the FP&E the Youngstown & Southern was rather drab, using two SW7 switchers it leased from a Pennsylvania shortline, the Montour Railroad. The Y&S was originally an electric interurban operation. It operated a little over 35 miles of track between Youngstown and Darlington, Pennsylvania, but most of its business was on the Youngstown end of the line. At Boardman, 5.5 miles south of Youngstown, SW7 71 passed the abandoned sub-station along Southern Boulevard in June 1969.

(Left & Below) The interurban heritage of the Y&S is evident in these two shots of the 71 working along Southern Boulevard in Boardman. It switched a siding north of Route 224 and then headed south alongside the boulevard in June 1969.

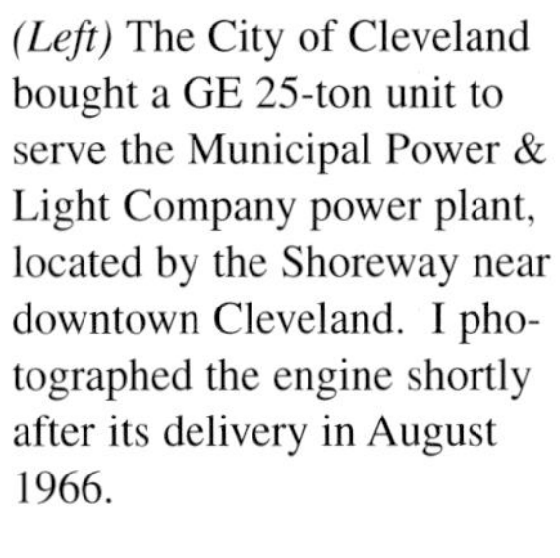
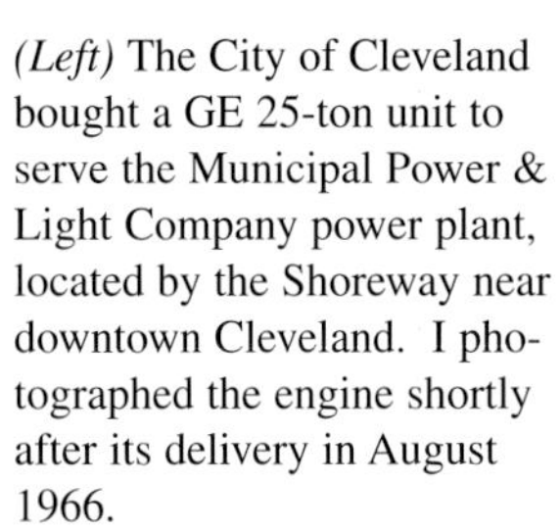

(Left) The City of Cleveland bought a GE 25-ton unit to serve the Municipal Power & Light Company power plant, located by the Shoreway near downtown Cleveland. I photographed the engine shortly after its delivery in August 1966.

(Below) Cleveland Electric Illuminating Company kept fireless cooker 7 in stand-by service at the Avon Lake power plant. It came alive for a Cleveland Railroad Club outing on May 24, 1970, putting out some nice white steam for the photographers.

(Above) The Illuminating Company, CEI, operated a fleet of GP38-2s in the 1980s. The company had the engines painted in a blue and yellow scheme inspired by the Santa Fe "yellow bonnet" scheme. Four of the CEI diesels were leading a pair of Conrail units on a westbound at Erie Street in Willoughby on March 15, 1980.

(Right) A westbound DE unit train crossed the Cuyahoga River Valley on the impressive Marcy Trestle, on the Short Line at Brooklyn Heights, Ohio in June 1974. A U30C led two SD40-2s on their way back to the Manor Branch of the Monongahela for loading.

(Below) Detroit Edison operated their own unit trains from the coal fields of Greene County, Pennsylvania on the Monongahela Railroad to their power plant at Monroe, Michigan. DE had both GE and EMD units painted in a metallic blue and silver scheme. A westbound was moving through Berea, passing BE interlocking on May 9, 1976. Lead unit 019 was one of 11 U30Cs acquired by Detroit Edison for this service in the early 1970s.

(Right) An eastbound empty train with 007 leading followed the Mahoning River at Girard, Ohio on the C&P on May 21, 1973.

Cuyahoga Valley Railroad

(Right) The Cuyahoga Valley Railroad served the Jones & Laughlin Steel Corporation in Cleveland. Jones & Laughlin was a fairly late arrival to the steel industry in Cleveland, acquiring the assets of Otis Iron & Steel Company in 1942. A common carrier, the CV operated 11.39 miles of track in the city, and later picked up an additional 2.2 miles of track from the Newburgh & South Shore when that road went out of business in the mid-1980s. The Cuyahoga Valley operated a stable of EMD end-cab switchers. The 1283, a SW1200 built in 1957, was working at West 3rd Street Yard on August 18, 1972.

(Above) SW8 855 was the only one of its type on the CV. It was built as an EMD demonstrator numbered EMD 500, and was purchased by the CV in 1954. It has a bottle car in tow passing the Republic Steel blast furnace at West 3rd Street on January 11, 1986.

(Below) Thick haze was covering the Cuyahoga River Valley on March 18, 1978 as Cuyahoga Valley SW1200 1285 switched ingot cars at Jones & Laughlin Steel. By this date Jones & Laughlin had been acquired by holding company Ling-Temco-Vought, Incorporated, which merged Jones & Laughlin with Republic Steel in 1984. The Pershing-Clark Avenue Bridge was a safe vantage point to view and photograph steel mill operations like this.

(Below) Cuyahoga Valley 1284, a SW1200, received red, white and blue Bicentennial paint. Industrial Cleveland was not the best environment for a fancy engine like this, but it still seems clean two years after the Bicentennial, switching at West 3rd Street on June 18, 1978.

Republic Steel

(Above) Republic Steel was Cleveland's own steel manufacturer, headquartered in Cleveland and associated with two of Cleveland's most famous industrialists, Cyrus Eaton and William G. Mather. Republic Steel was created in 1930 through the merger of several smaller steel companies. It operated a collection of mills in Cleveland and other locations, including a large operation in Youngstown. The Cleveland Works was the largest of the company's eight steel plants. Its rail ownings included both a plant operation and a common carrier, the River Terminal Railroad, in Cleveland. EMD 344 led an Alco at the company's Campbell Road facility on March 26, 1967.

(Above) The River Terminal operated 27.5 miles of trackage in Cleveland. Its roster included a variety of EMD switchers and one Alco S1. River Terminal pre-dated the formation of Republic Steel, having been started in 1909 by a predecessor steel company, Corrigan-McKinney Steel. The road was acquired by Republic in 1935. It not only served the mills directly but also served as a switching line interchanging with the major railroads around Cleveland. Two of the EMDs, SW900s 98 and 100, were switching at Campbell Road on June 18, 1978.

(Above & Right) Taking photographs of steel mill railroads isn't easy. An overhead location on public property helps. A pair of shots from an overhead vantage point on the Pershing Avenue Bridge shows the intricate trackwork at the Republic Steel complex. Republic's Bicentennial unit showed more of the grime from the hard work of switching the industrial complex in the Cuyahoga Valley flats. The two shots were taken on March 18, 1978. In 1984, Republic merged with Jones & Laughlin to form the LTV Steel Division of LTV Corporation, and the River Terminal Railway also became an LTV subsidiary.

Newburgh & South Shore

(Left) The busiest of Cleveland's steel mill railroads was the Newburgh & South Shore. The N&SS was a 7-mile U. S. Steel road that connected with most of the major mills along the Cuyahoga River in Cleveland. Its shops and offices were at East 71st Street in Cleveland. It also connected with the major railroads in Cleveland; in this shot from February 4, 1968 S2 1003 crossed the PRR at Harvard Tower.

(Below) The N&SS used the B&O bridge over the Cuyahoga to reach the American Steel & Wire complex at old Broadway. One of the major jobs of the road was to move hot metal and slag from the AS&W furnaces. On September 12, 1971 S2 1005 had a southbound heading over the bridge en route to the Cuyahoga Works at East 49th Street. The track crossing in the foreground is the N&W's former W&LE line from Campbell Road Yard to the EL yard at Literary Street on the ore dock line. The Cuyahoga Works closed in 1984, spelling the end for the N&SS's major source of traffic and the line ceased operation in 1986.

(Left) The 1011 switched slag cars at American Steel & Wire on February 4, 1973. American Steel & Wire was a U. S. Steel property that became a subsidiary of the giant corporation put together by Andrew Carnegie around the turn of the century. In 1907 USS built the Cuyahoga Works in Cuyahoga Heights. Beginning in the 1960s, U. S. Steel began to cut back its operations in Cleveland in favor of newer plants in other parts of the country.

(Below) The N&SS was planning a locomotive purchase in 1968. Two Bessemer & Lake Erie SD7s, the 451 and 452, were tested but found to be too large and heavy for the line. The two SDs, with the 452 leading long-end forward, departed the N&W's Campbell Yard for the N&SS's East 71st Yard on June 9, 1968. The B&LE had received ownership of the N&SS from U. S. Steel in 1951, so it was not surprising to see the B&LE try out some of its aging first-generation power on the smaller road.

(Left) To answer its locomotive needs, the Newburgh & South Shore purchased T6 switchers 1016 and 1017 from Alco in 1969. These were the last domestic diesel locomotives built by Alco. The duo were nearly new as they posed for me at the East 71st Yard on March 29, 1969. They ended what had been a long relationship between the road and Alco, beginning with the purchase of two HH1000 high-hood switchers in 1939.

AROUND THE REGION

(Above) The Lake Terminal Railroad served the U. S. Steel complex at Lorain, Ohio, west of Cleveland on the lake. As was typical of the U. S. Steel companies, the Lake Terminal's roster shifted often as engines were moved around the USS network of lines. Three units were lined up at the Lorain engine terminal on August 3, 1986; the Alco and Baldwin bear the emblem of USS. The Lake Terminal's own roster included only EMD units. The Lake Terminal operated 4.78 miles between Lorain and South Lorain.

(Below) Lima-Hamilton diesels were Ohio's own contribution to America's railroads, and the limited output of Lima products seemed to stay within the Buckeye State in large measure. Copperweld Steel at Warren, Ohio operated two Lima-Hamilton switchers. I was only permitted to take photos from the employee parking lot of the plant when I visited on June 14, 1975. The crew of the 9 obliged by pulling up to my location for photos. Thanks for the smoke on the reverse move back to the mill!

(Above) Another steel mill operator in the Youngstown area was Youngstown Sheet & Tube. Alco S1 664 rested at the old Division Street crossing at Youngstown on February 18, 1968.

(Above) Carbon Limestone operated a quarry at Hillsville, Pennsylvania on the Ohio/Pennsylvania state border. Limestone is an essential ingredient in steel making, so the demand for the white rock in the region was strong. The operation used narrow gauge switcher D-4 to work the tipple in January 1964. Carbon Limestone was served by a connection with a Pittsburgh & Lake Erie branch from Gateway Yard. The snow on the ground added more white to the white dust from the quarry that coated the tipple.

(Left) Carbon Limestone standard gauge switcher D-12 was a 60-ton General Electric unit with a road switcher style car body. It was at Hillsville in January 1964.

Diesel Powered Trips

(Above) PA1s 860 and 861 paused at Shenango Junction in Greenville, Pennsylvania, 38 miles east of Youngstown, on February 20, 1966. They handled a National Railway Historical Society passenger special from Akron that was being interchanged with the Bessemer & Lake Erie, which was then taking the special north to Erie, Pennsylvania.

(Right) In July of 1968 the Pittsburgh Chapter of the NRHS operated a fan trip with B&O RDC cars from Pittsburgh to Zanesville, Ohio. During the lunch break at Zanesville a number of the passengers took the opportunity to shoot the train near the brick Zanesville depot on Market and 2nd streets. Zanesville, a charming old Ohio city located where the Licking and Muskingum rivers converge, was the point at which two B&O lines met: an east/west line from Pittsburgh and Wheeling and a north/south line from Parkersburg, West Virginia. It was also served by lines of the Wheeling & Lake Erie and Pennsylvania.

Golden Spike Centennial

(Above) Cleveland area railfans were fortunate to be able to view main line steam operations well after they had vanished in other parts of the country. The Nickel Plate retained its splendid 2-8-4s on the Buffalo-Chicago main line through Cleveland into the late 1950s. So it was fitting that restored Nickel Plate Berkshire 759 return under steam to the former NKP main line in 1969. In May of 1969 the *Golden Spike Centennial Limited* operated from New York City to Ogden, Utah for the celebration of the completion of the first transcontinental railroad at Promontory Point, Utah in 1869. The train ran from New York to Kansas City, Missouri behind the restored 759. Back to the line it worked for so many years, the 759 headed west along 19th Street in Erie, Pennsylvania on May 4, 1969, racing the bicyclists on the famous stretch of main line street-running.

(Left) The 759 spent an overnight stay at Cleveland Union Terminal on May 4/5th, 1969. This was the last appearance of a live steam locomotive at CUT.

(Below) After resting at Cleveland, the 759 was back on the line on the morning of May 5. In the early dawn light the 759 steamed over the Rocky River Bridge at Rocky Ridge, Ohio, the beautiful lines of the 2-8-4 accentuated by back lighting.

Nickel Plate 765

(Above) Nickel Plate Berkshire 765 received minor repairs on September 9, 1990 at the main erecting hall at the Lima Locomotive Works at Lima, Ohio. It is seen here on the track where final assembly took place before the locomotive was test run and painted.

(Left) One of Lima's finest, Nickel Plate 765 debuted at New Haven, Indiana on September 22, 1979. The Nickel Plate Historical & Technical Society convention was in Fort Wayne, Indiana that weekend for the festive celebration honoring the beautifully restored 2-8-4.

(Below) The Fort Wayne Railroad Historical Society spent several years restoring the 765. The society assembled a short freight train of refrigerator cars and old Lake Erie & Western caboose for the inaugural run, which I photographed at New Haven, Indiana on September 22, 1979.

(Left) Later on September 8, 1982 the 765 accelerated past the grain elevators at Fostoria, Ohio.

(Left) The Southern Railway needed a new locomotive for its fall 1982 steam excursion schedule. Nickel Plate 765 was at Bellevue, Ohio and was available for service. It left Bellevue for Cincinnati with a 31-car freight train and an ex-Nickel Plate GP30 for protection. It departed Bellevue on the cold morning of September 8, 1982. The chilly morning air produced a beautiful plume of white exhaust as the engine started its train over the Center Street crossing.

(Left) In 1985 the 765 operated a number of fantrips in northeast Ohio. Several runs were made between Orrville, Ohio and Pittsburgh, Pennsylvania on the former PRR main line. It was crossing the Tuscarawas River at Massillon on the eastbound run on May 19, 1965.

(Left) The 765 was also the power for trips on the Pittsburgh & Lake Erie between Pittsburgh and Struthers, Ohio in spring 1985. It was near the Ohio/Pennsylvania border heading east on May 25, 1985.

(Right) On June 1, 1985 the 765 was running east along the Mahoning River at Lowellville, Ohio. The tracks in the foreground are the Baltimore & Ohio's Akron Main Line Subdivision, which paralleled the P&LE between Youngstown and New Castle, Pennsylvania.

Modern Steam of the C&O and N&W

(Right) The Nickel Plate Berkshires were the most appropriate restored steam locomotives to work around Cleveland, their old stomping ground. But other modern steam engines also livened up the local scene in the 1980s and 1990s. The Chesapeake & Ohio's 4-8-4 614 was eastbound at Center Street in Youngstown on June 27, 1981. In one of the strongest indications of how things can change over time, the huge Republic Steel mill seen here in the background, once a foundation of Youngstown's steel industry, has been torn down and the land is now a field. The complicated junction of past years has also been realigned.

(Left) The pre-1964 Norfolk & Western never made it to Cleveland, but it did get to Columbus. Its main line freights on the Scioto Division were handled by its Class A 2-6-6-4 articulated locomotives. One of the As, the 1218, was restored in the 1980s and operated over the Norfolk Southern system. On August 7, 1988 the glossy black engine handled a Buffalo to Bellevue, Ohio excursion on the former Nickel Plate. It was crossing the Cleveland drawbridge at Abbey Avenue with the Cleveland skyline in the distance.

(Right) The other Norfolk & Western locomotive under steam in the 1980s was J-class 4-8-4 611. The streamlined J crossed the Rocky River on August 3, 1985. Unlike the Cuyahoga, the Rocky River was not the haunt of lake boats but rather of leisure craft. The blue waters of Lake Erie are visible directly above the 611 as it heads west.

(Left) This is my last shot of the Norfolk Southern steam program. The 611 was westbound at Abbey Avenue on July 30, 1994. Just to the left of the drawbridge you can see the lights of the Cleveland Indians' new stadium, Jacobs Field, an important part of the restoration of downtown Cleveland in the past two decades.

Shaker Heights Rapid Transit

(Right) Our final section looks at the rapid transit lines around Cleveland. Shaker Rapid line car OX was at the scene of a wire break on Shaker Boulevard, east of Coventry Road, in Shaker Heights on March 23, 1968. The Shaker Heights Rapid Transit line dated back to the first decades of the 20th century, as the Van Sweringens connected their real estate developments in Shaker Heights with the city of Cleveland. At the time this shot was taken, the Shaker Rapid was owned and operated by the City of Shaker Heights.

(Above) Shaker Rapid car 12 was built by G. C. Kuhlman in 1914. It was heading west on Shaker Boulevard at Attleboro Road in Shaker Heights on February 11, 1968.

(Left) PCC car 95 was the last car built new for the Shaker Rapid, built by Pullman in 1947. It was westbound at Woodhill Road in Cleveland in January 1968. Crane car 0710 was stabilizing a damaged catenary pole on this winter day.

(Right) Eastbound 52 was at Shaker Square on January 5, 1975. The 52 was ex-Twin Cities car 341. Shaker Heights was the brainchild of the Van Sweringen brothers, who envisioned an affluent community linked to downtown Cleveland by rapid transit (owned by the brothers, needless to say). Their vision led to the creation of Shaker Heights in the early years of the 20th century, a model suburban community for the affluent. Shaker Square was actually in the city of Cleveland, on the border with Shaker Heights. Considered the second oldest shopping center development in the nation (Kansas City, Missouri claims the honor of the first), Shaker Square was built between 1927 and 1929 at the intersection of Shaker Boulevard and Moreland Boulevard, where the two lines of the Shaker Rapid converged. Shaker Square was more a "square" in the sense of a community center or meeting ground than in its actual shape, which is an octagon, reputedly modeled after a royal square in Copenhagen, Denmark.

(Right) Car 53 was heading west on Shaker Boulevard at the junction with the Van Aken Boulevard line on January 5, 1975. The Shaker Rapid system was built in three phases. From 1913 to 1915 to Shaker Square on the Shaker Boulevard and Van Aken Boulevard lines; in 1920 from Shaker Square to East 34th Street in Cleveland; and in 1930 to Terminal Tower.

(Left) Westbound car 61 crossed the short turn loop at Warrensville Center Road in Shaker Heights on October 23, 1975.

(Below) The far eastern end of the Shaker-Green Road line is rural and wooded. The yellow paint of a westbound Shaker Rapid car stood out against the deep snow as it neared Belvoir Boulevard in Shaker Heights on February 3, 1980.

(Left) Wearing the green paint of its former operator, the Illinois Terminal, PCC 451 stopped at the Lynnfield Road station in Shaker Heights on May 19, 1978. The car was leased from the Connecticut Electric Railway Association to handle increased ridership resulting from the formation of the new Regional Transit Authority. It last ran on the IT's commuter operation in St. Louis in 1959.

(Left) A rainbow of color was displayed by the collection of cars at the Warrensville yard in Shaker Heights on May 19, 1978.

(Below) Cleveland Transit System sold some of its cars to the Toronto, Ontario system in the early 1950s. Several returned to Cleveland after the formation of the new Regional Transit Authority. The inaugural run of two former Toronto cars was on October 20, 1978. The cars were short-turning on the loop at Shaker Square showing off the new RTA emblem.

(Right) Cleveland Transit System car 70 was decorated in Christmas colors with a wreath around the headlight in the Christmas season in 1985. The paint job was authorized by the American Greeting Card Company and incorporated some of their trademark characters. The car was heading east on Van Aken Boulevard at Avalon Road in Shaker Heights on December 21, 1985.

Cleveland Transit System

(Right) Cleveland Transit System line car 024 was originally Shaker Rapid car 17. A G. C. Kuhlman product from 1914, it is seen at the Windermere Shops in East Cleveland on May 24, 1964. The line to Windermere from CUT opened on March 15, 1955, a distance of 7.8 miles.

(Below) The original Cleveland Transit System 100 and 200 series cars were built by St. Louis Car Company in 1954. A four-car train turned on the loop track at Windermere station in January 1966. The CTS used overhead catenary to provide electricity to the cars.

(Left) The west end of the CTS Rapid was extended in stages between 1955 and 1968: first to West 117th Street in 1955, then to West Park, Lorain Avenue, in 1958. The line was extended to Cleveland Hopkins International Airport in 1968. Before the extension I got this shot of the West Park terminal on February 26, 1967.

(Above) A westbound four-car train was heading to the airport at Mayfield Road on January 19, 1975.

(Left) A four-car train was heading west rounding the curve at East 34th Street on April 13, 1976.

(Above) Let's go back in time for our final shot of railroading in Cleveland. The premier passenger train through Cleveland was the Central's 20TH CENTURY LIMITED. The CENTURY passed through Cleveland well after dark in both directions, as it was timed for an end-of-business day departure and morning arrival at its termini in Chicago and Manhattan. The eastbound CENTURY, train #26, stopped at Collinwood for water and fuel around 11:30 PM. With the last run of the train just weeks away, a night photo session was a must, and was set for a night in late November 1967. My best friend Al Clum worked the camera while I used the Gossen Luna-Six light meter to get the time exposure information. Managing the meter, a stopwatch, and a flashlight all at once was a real challenge on this night, but shooting the end of the legendary train and its famous observation cars and lighted train sign made it all worthwhile.

Even though trains like the CENTURY are long gone, in 2005 as this is published, Cleveland remains a focal point of railroad activity. It's down now to two major roads – the Norfolk Southern and CSX – but together they use Cleveland as a key hub of activity, linking their lines between the Northeast and Midwest. The breakup of Conrail in 1999 highlighted the importance of Cleveland, as the two big roads had to find ways to divide up the Conrail trackage through Cleveland in a way that made sense to each. In the broader region we've looked at, the rail action is enriched by regional Wheeling & Lake Erie (with a route that is not identical to the old W&LE of Nickel Plate days) and the tourist railroad Cuyahoga Valley Scenic that operates part of the old B&O Valley Line in the spectacular scenery along the Cuyahoga River south of Cleveland. The Rapid Transit system still links the suburbs to downtown. All in all, the Cleveland area is still a great place to watch trains.

Thanks for allowing me to show you around town!
Dave McKay